The CATHOLIC CHALLENGE:

A Question

of

Conscience

THOMAS W. REZANKA

THE CATHOLIC CHALLENGE:
A Question of Conscience
BY THOMAS W. REZANKA

Published by:

Better World Together Publishing Co.
Post Office Box 2015
Palm Harbor, Florida 34682-2015

Orders may be placed @ TheCatholicChallenge.com

Copyright © 2004 by Thomas W. Rezanka

ISBN 0-9762100-0-2

TABLE OF CONTENTS

INTRODUCTION

If after reading this book, you take issue with some of the author's positions, at least be honest in your criticism. Compliment what is good, worthwhile or thought provoking. Remember that many Catholics, especially those who have sought leadership roles within the Church and who understand the importance of the God given gift of reason, often share the same views as those which are expressed within this writing.

In order to understand the challenge and how it must be answered, both by the ordained as well as by the laity, it is important to read and understand each of the prefaces. IT IS PARTICULARLY IMPORTANT FOR THE CLERGY TO READ EACH OF THE PREFACES, BUT IN PARTICULAR, PREFACE No. 4.

All scriptural citations come from *The New American Bible,* © 1970 by the Confraternity of Christian Doctrine, Washington, D.C., including *The Revised New Testament,* © 1986, by the Confraternity of Christian Doctrine.

PREFACE NO. 1

WHAT YOU NEED TO KNOW
ABOUT THIS BOOK

The concept for this book has been in my thoughts for over five years. It has not been precipitated by any one event nor by any several events. Its motivation has come from the depths of my soul; a heartfelt yearning to see Christ's Church further grow in order to serve the increasing needs of its people. Although Catholics number in excess of one billion throughout the world, the Church's current leadership has demonstrated a distinctly distant, uncaring and unacceptable disdain for its parishioners as well as for their spiritual leaders, those priests who seek neither power nor prestige, but merely to serve Christ by serving others. In the United States alone, it is estimated that in the last 25 years over 25,000 priests have voluntarily left the priesthood and hundreds of thousands, perhaps millions of lay people have left for non-denominational congregations or have stopped practicing their faith altogether. When you speak with these or even others still within the Church, you immediately identify certain common feelings of frustration or betrayal. Whether entirely accurate or not, the reactions are real, the feelings not without basis. Some are reflected in the following thoughts from various parishioners who belong to churches both within and outside of my own diocese:

(1) I made a suggestion to our Pastor that it might be a good idea in the intercessionary prayers to pray for our men and women overseas, and he looked right through me as if I didn't exist.

(2) Over a period of three months, I left notes in the church suggestion box mentioning that of approximately twenty parishes I have either visited or been a parishioner in, that no church building was ever so uncomfortably warm as this one and asked, "Could you please do something to fix the air conditioning." The Pastor's response was to take the suggestion boxes out of the Church.

(3) I suggested to the Pastor that the car parking stops (made from cement) which were installed many years ago when the Church was built, were more of a liability than a necessity as a number of parishioners have tripped over them in the early morning and evening hours when they are harder to see. He ignored the suggestion until one day a parishioner

tripped over one and broke his hip.

(4) I have served on my Parish's finance committee and I know for a fact that a former priest embezzled $240,000 from this parish. There is no accountability.

(5) I and others went to the Bishop to complain about our Pastor's breach of his vow of celibacy. We were told that it would be investigated. Twelve months later nothing has been done.

(6) We have complained to the Bishop about the many ways in which our Pastor has and continues to alienate our parishioners. He simply tells us that he has no one to send in his place.

(7) As a former priest, I left the priesthood in order to marry and as much to be rid of the deviants (priests) who were assigned to my rectory.

(8) I'll never go to confession again. The priest made me feel as though I was the worst person in the world, yet I neither committed murder nor was adulterous.

(9) Our new Pastor has removed the pews and kneelers in our church and has taken the figure of Christ off of the cross. We now stand throughout the Mass and visitors ask us if this is really a Roman Catholic Church.

(10) The priest refused to marry us because we hadn't completed the Pre-Cana course. We weren't kids. We were both married before and lost our spouses.

(11) Our Pastor could make the concrete walls cry from boredom. If he is incapable of making the word of the Lord come alive, can't he get someone to speak in his place?

(12) The following is an excerpt from a letter to one particular parishioner's Pastor, which the parishioner shared with me after he and others were summarily "fired" by their Pastor from their parish council. Without any forewarning, or prior notice to any of them, the Pastor simply walked into the parish council meeting and stated, "I am adopting a new rule that anyone who has served on the parish council for two years or more, this is the last meeting for you." Part of the letter from one of those parishioners to his Pastor reads as follows: "It would have been basic common courtesy for you to have contacted each of us prior to that meeting to let it be known that you were going to immediately and unilaterally institute a two-year term for members of the parish council and immediately dismiss those who had served at least two years. It would also have been basic common courtesy, even if you didn't mean it, to thank the people whom you would

be dismissing from the council for their service, considering the fact that they are volunteers who take time away from their families to help the parish." [The entire letter is printed as an exhibit to the section within Chapter IV entitled "How the Ordained Must Help."]

Other examples could be given, but what purpose would they serve. The Church leadership will undoubtedly assert that these things are all in the past, or that the deficiencies of a few men can't be held against the entire Church, or that these criticisms are merely the ruminations of malcontents within the Church, who don't even belong in the Church. This last assertion will most likely be their first inclination, as it was just recently when I took a chance and opened myself up to a priest whom I had just met. I summarized for him why I felt the Church needed to change: the refusal for so long to take child abuse seriously; the intentional actions taken to hide it or ignore it; the clergy's lack of accountability to its parishioners; the impatience we feel as members of the Body of Christ, because everything is dictated from the top down; how the current structure leaves no room for appeal; how Bishops can rule arbitrarily within their respective dioceses; how Bishops can make themselves inaccessible or simply ignore whatever they don't consider to be a problem; and how the Catholic Church has not necessarily evolved in a way most pleasing to Christ.

You know that this priest looked me square in the eye and said "So why don't you just leave the Church?" This unfortunately may well be the response of those in authority within the Church. Should you criticize their conduct, their rules, regulations, or their decisions, you may quickly find yourself referred to as a Gnostic, heretic, blasphemer, or someone who should be denied communion or excommunicated, all under the guise of protecting the faith, but with the hidden agenda of merely protecting their own positions and power. Their view of the laity is that we could never be touched by the Holy Spirit or ever understand what Christ wants for his Church on earth. No, this is reserved for those men, whether truly called to the priesthood or not, who have risen through the ranks to become Monsignors, Bishops and Cardinals. In the business world, we have a saying: "It's not only the cream that rises to the top." Absolute power is most corruptive when left unchecked and when the leadership within our Church no longer embraces Christ's teachings, then we, the Body of

Christ, must act to correct the mistakes which have been made. How do we know whether our leadership is acting for themselves and for their own self-interest? We need only measure their actions by Christ's teachings. Do they by their actions treat (love) their neighbors as they treat (love) themselves (or is there a double standard)? Do their actions show their love for others as did Christ's sacrifice on the cross for all of our sins? Christ was willing to forgive thieves, tax collectors and prostitutes. Do they by their actions demonstrate forgiveness and understanding or are these things reserved by them to themselves only?

As Catholics we understand that judgment will be passed upon us by Jesus alone. Unlike the modern day Pharisee, who may travel under the label of Born-Again Christian we do not judge other Christians to be unworthy of salvation. We understand that the world around us is becoming more secular and we are appalled by this. We also understand that whether we have verbalized it or not, the present organizational/leadership model within the Church has failed; that clergy, in general, are not born leaders, and the laity has for far too long been looked upon as the worker bees who serve only to contribute their money and sweat, but to otherwise not be taken seriously. This book proposes another way and can either be embraced by the clergy, which will bring a brighter future, or can be attacked by the clergy, which unfortunately will add further to the continuing decline of the organized Church.

I have served on several parish councils under different Pastors, and have examined revenues and sources of contributions, as well as have spoken to Pastors in other parishes to make certain that the observations of our parish were not atypical. Our experience taught us that a mere 20% of parishioners were carrying the financial burden of our parish, while the rest gave little or nothing at all. The clergy finds acceptable that they have only reached one out of five Catholics and the rest are left to their own self-concern and selfishness. Instructive to us all, Christ tells the parable about the shepherd who having lost one sheep leaves the 99 behind in search of it. Yet the clergy we have today are satisfied that only 20% understand their relationship to God and the responsibilities which flow from that relationship. The current model isn't working.

The purpose of this book is to suggest that Christ's Church on earth is meant to grow, to evolve, and to change in order to meet the needs of His people. The changes, not in dogma, but in presentation, which took place under Vatican II, reflect this nature. At a time within human history, when we are faced with the greatest physical dangers and the greatest moral dilemmas of all time, the church, through its clergy, working hand in hand with its people, must provide enlightened spiritual guidance. Speaking as a member of the laity we believe there is a better way, and that we are a part of that better way. At present (the Church through its current leadership), is failing to do what needs to be done, primarily because the dictates of those within the hierarchy ignore the selflessness, the mercy, and the love which Christ showed, when he walked among us. This can be considered a momentary aberration if we stand up and allow our voices, our hearts, and our minds to be counted. All we need to say is that we believe there is a better way, and we are a part of that better way.

PREFACE NO. 2

The Body of Christ has at least two meanings within the Church. The first, that in celebration of the Eucharist during Mass, the communion wafer literally becomes Christ present to His disciples within the Church. In the second usage, the Body of Christ refers to the body of the Church, Christ's people here on earth. It is to the second Body of Christ that this work is directed. The human development of the Church has occurred over two thousand years and Christ left it in the hands of its first leader, The Apostle Peter, also the first Pope, on whose shoulders He indicated that He would build His Church. Christ's Church, the Catholic (meaning universal) church has grown to over one billion followers across the globe. As with any immense organization, a hierarchy of Bishops, Cardinals, Monsignors, as well as church Pastors, has evolved by which to govern it. This form of government from the top down almost entirely excludes the Body of Christ, Christ's people, without whom (as without Christ) there would be no Church. It is suggested that the time has come to revisit where the organizational authority, not the teaching authority, should lie, although sometimes even teachers fall prey to their own prejudices and agenda.

PREFACE NO. 3

When reading this book you may be tempted to conclude that it is an attack upon the Catholic Church.

On the contrary, it is a call to the Church, its religious and laity to remember that Christ did not come to establish one thousand Christian churches, but only one, which, over time has become known as the Catholic Church. It is this Church which I shall refer to as "the Church" through this book and it is this Church which must re-assert itself as the champion of Christ on earth. To do this, the Church must challenge itself first and then others second. The first challenge requires the Church to elevate the baptized and confirmed but un-ordained to a more equal role within the Church.

PREFACE NO. 4

This book is dedicated to the many wonderful priests within the Church who have truly responded to their calling in life. They have unselfishly committed themselves to ministering to Christ's people; often accepting a vow of poverty, dedicated only to preaching the Word of God and helping whenever and wherever possible God's people. References in this book to "the ordained" and to "the clergy" are normally not references to them, but only to those who have sought and obtained positions of authority within the Church and who, although they will not admit it to themselves, are filled with dead men's bones, pursuing not Christ's work on earth but only their own agenda. They have ears but do not listen; eyes but do not see, and voices which do not speak, except to defend the status quo.

For the priests to whom this book is dedicated, it offers another way. One which is more open and true to itself, one which is not based upon politics, one which does not selfishly pursue the maintenance of power, and one which will finally aid you in your work. Look beyond my anger and my frustration and you will see it.

This Page Intentionally Left Blank

CHAPTER I:
URGENT NEED FOR CHANGE

Throughout history, men and women have adopted sayings, which we refer to as truisms, because our human experience has taught that they are generally accepted as correct. One of those truisms is that "Absolute Power Corrupts Absolutely." The clergy and laity should both consider this when examining the recent and long-term history of the Church.

The Church, not unlike a large corporation, has a definite hierarchy with the Pope in Rome sitting as its Chief Executive Officer. The Bishop and Archbishops have their own little fiefdoms because of the amount of authority delegated to them by the Pope. The Bishops are like Senior Vice Presidents, who within certain limitations, are permitted to run their own departments with little interference from Rome. It is because of this and the lack of lay oversight that one man may within his own Diocese overrule advisors, take inappropriate actions and interfere with the work of Christ, if he so chooses to do so. As Catholics, we know that Christ sees things as they are, but we are left with little recourse in this world because this closed and self-regulating governing body is unlikely to be swayed by our concerns or complaints. Would the current crisis within the Church, where the crimes of priests against their parishioners and the children of those parishioners, have been covered up, sometimes for decades, or even occurred if the laity were exercising a supervisory role within their dioceses? I think not.

The urgent need for change, although highlighted by the cases of pedophilia and sexual abuse, is far more insidious, growing within the Church much like a virus, as Christ's people, after centuries of neglect begin to question their lack of meaningful participation. A growing frustration within the Church has swept through its parishioners, who view the Church, with the exception of Christ Himself, as uncaring, unsympathetic, and unaccountable. If for example, you complain that you cannot hear yourself think once you have received communion, because the choir is singing, you are rebuffed with the assertion that the music or singing is called for at this juncture in the liturgy. And who established that liturgy and why are they so aghast at changing a portion of it which would allow Christ's people a quiet interlude to pray to Him during the celebration of His most magnanimous sacrifice? Why is it that common sense may not have its place within the Church? Of course, the response by the ordained will be that somehow, somewhere, in some Vatican II document, or some other church document, the sacrifice of the Mass must be carried out in this fashion. Someone like me should not have to write a book complaining of such practice before this information becomes common place or before the liturgy is changed to permit the laity the silence which they require to worship their God, without the necessity of having that silence interrupted by the singing of songs. Perhaps a simple change to playing music softly would be sufficient. Where parishioners are not attempting to change the teachings of Christ, the final say over such matters should reside in the parish councils, not in the Pastor, who may not be in agreement with the desires of his parishioners. At present, the parish councils (when they exist within a parish) are advisory bodies, with the sole decision-making authority vested only in the Pastor. Excuse me! The Pastor is one person. The parish council may consist of 12 or more representatives of the parish community. Who will have a better grasp of community sentiment, the twelve who are a part of the community or the one who has been placed there by the Bishop?

The Church works through its appointed Pastors and vests authority in them. Accountability, if any, begins and ends with the priest who is the Pastor. In many parishes the Pastor appoints all or many of the members of the parish council. When there is a Finance Committee, the members of this committee are most often appointed by the Pastor. What if the Priest himself is the thief, or lacks business acumen? Should not the parishioners be authorized within their Church community to supervise their offerings? Why must the Pastor be given so much authority with so little mandated lay supervision? The Pastor and priest should be a man of God, called to his profession from above. He needs to minister to the sick, to the confused and to others in need. There is no God-given rule that he must also be the parish administrator and very often a parish will have an administrator or business manager. However, he or she will always be selected and employed by the Pastor. Since the parish council should be involved in the administration of its parish, there is no reason why the council could not be authorized to do the hiring and firing of the parish administrators and the business managers so long as the Pastor's sentiments regarding a particular candidate or employee are taken into consideration.

If you within the clergy don't believe what I'm saying to you, then perhaps you should reflect upon the many studies which have been done both within and outside the Church, with respect to sacrificial giving. Those who have conducted these studies, and this can be confirmed by those who direct stewardship in your parishes, hold the belief that Catholic Christians generally give less per person to their churches then do their fellow Christians. Do you, who are Priests, Bishops and Cardinals, ever consider that when you dictate everything from the top down, you do not make your parishioners stakeholders in your enterprise. When they feel that you are unaccountable to them, when you ignore suggestions from a viable number of parishioners, or fail to act upon your own parish census or questionnaire, how do you expect your parishioners to take seriously the concept of sacrificial giving? Granted that sacrificial giving or stewardship must also be spiritually based and embraced, how can you expect more when you have for so long disenfranchised the very people from whom you desire financial support?

Then, as if to add insult to injury, and further undermine

the laity's faith in your leadership, you Bishops within the United States issued a statement on Friday, June 16, 2004 entitled "Catholics in Political Life,"[1] likely to be looked upon as the single most significant mistake ever made by United States Catholic Bishops, only to be exceeded by the covering up of child abuse within the Church and the reassignment of sexual deviants to other parishes without notice given to those parishes. The present perception is that this body within the Church has lost its way, but because of their current positions, must immediately rescind this statement.

When the Pharisees attempted to trap Jesus, they asked him, "Is it lawful to pay the census tax to Caesar or not?" Jesus said to them, "Show me the coin that pays the census tax." Then they handed him the Roman coin. He said to them, "Whose image is this and whose inscription? They replied, Caesar's." At that he said to them, "Then repay to Caesar what belongs to Caesar and to God what belongs to God." Mt 22, 17-22. Jesus never interfered with the civil authority of His time. Although the Jews were looking for a military messiah who would overthrow the civil government of the Romans, which they felt was oppressive, He never said, "Use my teachings to control political figures." The United

States was founded by people whose heartfelt belief was that there should be no state sponsored or approved religion, for without this prohibition, one church or another would grow in such power that it would dictate to the civil leaders what should be done, and then that country would have a defacto state religion. It is one thing to state that a Catholic's view of abortion, if contrary to the Church, should be re-examined. It is quite another to attempt to intrude into politics and civil governance by threatening political candidates with refusal of Holy Communion. Elsewhere in this book, I label the Born-Again Christian as the modern day Pharisee. It saddens me to the depths of my soul that our Bishops desire to compete for this title. As Church leaders, it is your responsibility to show by your actions humility, understanding, and forgiveness. You show no understanding of what a woman goes through when she is faced with this decision. If abortion is such a terrible thing, and certainly it can be, then why haven't you reached out more visibly and with more resources to those facing this decision, so that counseling and financial support could be provided to convince more women not to make this choice? Why instead do you seek to judge when Christ Himself has told you not to?

Does not Matthew say in Chapter 7, Verses 1 through 5 "Stop judging, that you may not be judged. For as you judge, so will you be judged, and the measure with which you measure will be measured out to you. Why do you notice the splinter in your brother's eye, but do not perceive the wooden beam in your own eye? How can you say to your brother, "Let me remove that splinter from your eye," while the wooden beam is in your own eye? You hypocrite, remove the wooden beam from your eye first; then you will see clearly to remove the splinter from your brother's eye." How can you possibly deny Holy Communion to political candidates who support a woman's right to make this decision? When you judge them unworthy to receive Holy Communion (your statement says that Bishops and Priests can deny Holy Communion to these people) you are judging what is in a person's heart. How can you know what is in a person's heart? Such a judgment is reserved to Jesus Christ Himself and not to you. How can any priest see into anyone's heart? How could any member of the clergy presume to know only what Jesus knows? This is where the folly of your statement lies. You are so focused on the evil of abortion that you have allowed Satan himself to draw you into the trap of fanaticism.

Since when are crises of conscience to be resolved by legislation rather than by the penitent sinner alone in communication with his or her Savior? Abortion is an extremely important issue, not just to the Church, but to society in general; it is not one to be decided solely by a group of men who themselves have never been faced by the decision. There are times when as a result of rape, incest, or threat of death to the mother, it cannot be said with any moral certitude that abortion is clearly against the will of God. If freedom of choice is as essential to Christian theology as it is, for only with freedom of choice can one understand the difference between good and evil, then when there is no choice, when the will is overcome by someone else, as in rape or incest, it cannot be said that abortion is then morally objectionable. How do we know this? Because none of us are perfect, not you, not me, not the clergy, and not our legislators. Because we are imperfect and cannot know the mind of God, we have no right to use religion to threaten politicians or to interfere with political discussions which must take place on this most important issue.

As much as Catholics may wish to see the elimination of abortions, we must consider that we are dealing with two lives here, that of the mother as well as of the child which she is carrying. We cannot on the basis of religion, simply ignore her rights and elevate those of her unborn child beyond hers. That is why this issue is so difficult, both to discuss and to resolve. As much as we would like to protect the life of the unborn child, how can we in good conscience use religion to legislate away a medical procedure which may be necessary to save the mother's life. This is an issue, as there are other issues in our lives, which cannot be adequately addressed by constitutional prohibitions or by legislation. They must be left to be resolved between the woman electing an abortion and her God, for we as Catholics know that it is not beyond the measure of Christ's love to forgive this woman the decision which she feels that she must make. This is a time for us to recognize our human frailty and fallibility; to recognize the fact that whether you are pro-life or pro-choice you may both ultimately be wrong, especially in the way that you treat each other.

CHAPTER II:

THE CHURCH IN HISTORY

A. WHY THE DIFFERENT CHRISTIAN DENOMINATIONS?

There have been so many books written in regard to the history of the Roman Catholic Church, that it is hard to know which ones to pay particularly close attention to and which ones to ignore entirely. Some authors have spent a good portion of their lives, and others their entire lives, writing about a history which covers over 2,000 years. It is not my objective here to attempt but the briefest of limited summaries. We should first recall that all of the early Christians were Jews and the fact that the faith was able to spread across the globe is nothing short of miraculous. The inception of the Catholic Church always begins with Jesus' calling of his initial twelve apostles. Luke 6, 13 and Mark 3, 13-19. It was necessary for Christ to choose one among these to lead the others, with the hope and expectation that this would eliminate divisions among them.

"Who do people say that the Son of Man is? They replied,

'Some say John the Baptist, others Elijah, still others Jeremiah or one of the prophets.' He said to them, 'But who do you say that I am?' Simon Peter said in reply, 'You are the Messiah, the Son of the living God.' Jesus said to him in reply, 'Blessed are you, Simon son of Jonah. For flesh and blood has not revealed this to you, but my heavenly Father. And so I say to you, you are Peter, and upon this rock I will build my church, and the gates of the netherworld shall not prevail against it." Mt 16, 14-18.

The view of the Catholic Church from within is that by reason of unbroken papal succession from the first Pope, Peter, to the current Pope, the Catholic Church is the only Church that Christ intended to establish. Although there is a certain amount of pride associated with being a member of the Church which Christ Himself established, it also means that we owe a greater responsibility to His teachings and to the responsibilities for carrying out those teachings faithfully.

In his book, *A Concise History of the Catholic Church*, Thomas Bokenkotter has this to say about the Church's history from approximately 312 AD until 461 AD: "The period from Constantine to Pope Leo the Great (461 AD) was one of decisive importance in the history of the Catholic Church.

Many of the basic features of Catholicism were fixed during these years in the form they were to retain, with relatively few modifications, for the next fifteen hundred years. Its chief act of worship, the Mass, was highly standardized and ritualized. Its chief dogma, the belief in Jesus Christ, God and Man, was affirmed and clarified in lasting terms. Many practices henceforth fundamental to its discipline and life originated and were incorporated into its canon law. Its clergy took on the character of a sacred caste and began to submit themselves to the law of celibacy. Monasticism took root in Egypt and spread across Christendom. Finally, the basic principles of its code of social and personal ethics achieved nearly permanent form." 2

Mr. Bokenkotter labels the period of 1300 AD to 1650 AD as "The Unmaking of Christendom."3 This is the historical period during which various movements occurred, not the least of which were Calvinism and Lutheranism, which ultimately resulted in divisions within the church. These protests against certain church directives became more generally known as Protestantism, with now many former Catholics calling themselves Lutherans, Presbyterians, Methodists, and by many other names.

B. THE CHURCH TODAY

Although the concept for this work was developed before the scandalous public discovery of child abuse and sexual molestation of children by those who said they were priests of Jesus Christ, if the laity, rather than the ordained, had been in charge of overseeing complaints by parishioners, complaints of any sort whatsoever, these dangerous predators would have been prosecuted or at least removed from their positions of opportunity many decades ago. For so long as the ordained falsely believe that only they are touched by the Holy Spirit, will the Church continue to wallow in indifference, a pale figure of what it should be today.

The scandal within the Church pertains as much to the conscious attempts to cover up the unacceptable behavior as it does to the unacceptable behavior. Why did this occur in Christ's own Church? How could it occur in the Church which Christ himself established? These questions are not all that different from the one which asks "Why do bad things happen to good people?" With respect to the Catholic Church, if you were Satan, which church would you attack, Christ's Church or one which claims to be Christ's Church. Would you go after Christ's priests (or the weakness in some) or would you attack some self-proclaimed minister who teaches his flock that unless you accept Jesus Christ as your personal Savior and are thereby "saved," you will not see the Kingdom of God. Satan need not attack this modern day Pharisee, for he is already condemned by his own words. He professes to speak for Christ while at the same time blaspheming the Holy Spirit. He does this by deciding that all other Christians are damned, without recognizing either the Spirit within them or the "Word" which teaches that you shall not judge others without subjecting yourself to the same judgment. If you were Satan and you wanted to taunt your creator, whom would you attack?

Even before the days of public scandal, the Church would ask for money from its parishioners but would rarely be accountable for that money. Accountability, if genuine, must not just report what money has been collected or what it was used for, but must seek the guidance of those who have contributed. The feeling within the Body of Christ has been, "Why should I contribute if you care not for how I would like to see this money spent?" Certainly, there are collections for specific purposes: retired priests, overseas missions, vocations, and others as to which we know the purpose and agree with it by contributing, but this is not entirely the case with general collection revenues. Shouldn't the Church involve us in its objectives and strive to make this sacrificial giving more personal for us? There is a different and better way. Democratization of the Church need not be a bad thing. Is not the Pope selected by democratic balloting? My mother was fond of stating, "What's good for the goose is good for the gander." The voices of the Body of Christ have been ignored for too long. How do we know this to be true? Ask yourself these questions:

✝   How successful have parishioners been when they have petitioned their Bishop for removal of a Priest who was unsuited for that particular (or any) parish?

✝   How often have parishioners gained access to their Bishop to discuss what they viewed as an important issue?

✝   How many petitions, letters or complaints to a Bishop have been intercepted and responded to by an intermediary for the Bishop?

✝   How many Bishops do you know who would be willing to delegate authority over monetary issues to any lay panel?

✝ Why are parish councils merely advisory with no real power (and perhaps worse, even optional)?

✝ Shouldn't parish councils be given express authority under canon law, over administrative matters, with members elected by the Body of Christ?

✝ Why should the members of the Body of Christ be treated with less dignity and less respect than their counterparts who are ordained and who hold positions of authority?

✝ Why is it so important to the ordained that they make every decision which affects the Church as a whole?

Throughout the New Testament, Jesus Christ speaks to these issues, which are now our concerns. Consider His instruction and His warnings:

"Enter through the narrow gate; for the gate is wide and the road broad that leads to destruction, and those who enter through it are many. How narrow the gate and constricted the road that leads to life. And those who find it are few." Mt 7, 13-14

"At that time the disciples approached Jesus and said, "Who is the greatest in the Kingdom of Heaven?" He called a child over, placed it in their midst, and said, "Amen, I say to you, unless you turn and become like children, you will not enter the kingdom of heaven. Whoever humbles himself like this child is the greatest in the kingdom of heaven. And whoever receives one child such as this in my name receives me." Mt 18, 1-5

"Then Jesus spoke to the crowds and to his disciples, saying "The scribes and the Pharisees have taken their seat on the chair of Moses. Therefore, do and observe all things whatsoever they tell you, but do not follow their example. For they preach, but they do not practice. They tie up heavy burdens and lay them on people's shoulders, but they will not lift a finger to move them. All their works are performed to be seen. They widen their phylacteries and lengthen their tassels. They love places of honor at banquets, seats of honor in synagogues, greetings in marketplaces, and the salutation "Rabbi." As for you, do not be called "Rabbi." You have but one teacher, and you are all brothers. Call no one on earth your father; you have but one Father in heaven. Do not be called "Master"; you have but one master, the Messiah. The greatest among you must be your servant. Whoever exalts himself will be humbled; but whoever humbles himself will be exalted." Mt 23,1-12 [Although we address our priests with a respectful salutation like "Good day, Father Paul," rather than using the title Reverend, we as Catholics understand the teachings of this chapter of Matthew and we are not calling anyone on earth our Father. We merely use the title "Father" in place of the alternate title of Reverend. We acknowledge that there is only one Father, who in turn sent the Son, who in turn sent the Holy Spirit, the Paraclete. If you belong to another Christian denomination and are not Catholic, do not let this custom separate you from us.]

"Everyone will be salted with fire. Salt is good, but if salt becomes insipid, with what will you restore its flavor? Keep salt in yourselves and you will have peace with one another." Mk 9, 49-50

"Jesus summoned them and said to them, "You know that those who are recognized as rulers over the Gentiles lord it over them, and their great ones make their authority over them felt. But it shall not be so among you. Rather, whoever wishes to be great among you will be your servant; whoever wishes to be first among you will be the slave of all. For the Son of Man did not come to be served but to serve and to give his life as a ransom for many." Mk 10, 42-45

"After this he appeared in another form to two of them

walking along on their way to the country. They returned
and told the others; but they did not believe them either.
[But] later, as the eleven were at table, he appeared to them
and rebuked them for their unbelief and hardness of heart
because they had not believed those who saw him after he
had been raised. He said to them, "Go into the whole world
and proclaim the gospel to every creature. Whoever believes
and is baptized will be saved; whoever does not believe will
be condemned." Mk 16, 12-16

"Then he said to all, "If anyone wishes to come after
me, he must deny himself and take up his cross daily and
follow me. For whoever wishes to save his life will lose it,
but whoever loses his life for my sake will save it. What profit
is there for one to gain the whole world yet lose or forfeit
himself? Whoever is ashamed of me and my words, the Son
of Man will be ashamed of when he comes in his glory and in
the glory of the Father and of the holy angels." Lk 9, 23-26

"An argument arose among the disciples about which of
them was the greatest. Jesus realized the intention of their
hearts and took a child and placed it by his side and said to
them, "Whoever receives this child in my name receives me,
and whoever receives me receives the one who sent me. For

the one who is least among all of you is the one who is the greatest." Lk 9, 46-48

"There is nothing concealed that will not be revealed, nor secret that will not be known. Therefore whatever you have said in the darkness will be heard in the light, and what you have whispered behind closed doors will be proclaimed on the housetops. I tell you, my friends, do not be afraid of those who kill the body but after that can do no more. I shall show you whom to fear. Be afraid of the one who after killing has the power to cast into Gehenna; yes, I tell you, be afraid of that one." Lk 12, 2-5

"Gird your loins and light your lamps and be like servants who await their master's return from the wedding, ready to open immediately when he comes and knocks. Blessed are those servants whom the master finds vigilant on his arrival. Amen, I say to you, he will gird himself, have them recline at table, and proceed to wait on them. And should he come in the second or third watch and find them prepared in this way, blessed are those servants. Be sure of this: If the master of the house had known the hour when the thief was coming, he would not have let his house be broken into. You also must be prepared for at an hour you do not expect, the Son of Man will come." Lk 12, 35-40

"He passed through towns and villages, teaching as he went and making his way to Jerusalem. Someone asked him "Lord will only a few people be saved"? He answered them, "Strive to enter through the narrow gate, for many, I tell you, will attempt to enter but will not be strong enough. After the master of the house has arisen and locked the door, then will you stand outside knocking and saying, "Lord, open the door for us." He will say to you in reply, "I do not know where you are from." And you will say, "We ate and drank in your company and you taught in our streets." Then he will say to you, "I do not know where [you] are from. Depart from me, all you evildoers!" And there will be wailing and grinding of teeth when you see Abraham, Isaac and Jacob and all the prophets in the kingdom of God and you yourselves cast out. And people will come from the east and the west and from the north and the south and will recline at table in the kingdom of God. For behold, some are last who will be first, and some are first who will be last." Lk 13, 22-30

"Salt is good, but if salt itself looses its taste, with what can its flavor be restored? It is fit neither for the soil nor for the manure pile; it is thrown out. Whoever has ears to hear ought to hear." Lk 14, 34-35

"The Pharisees, who loved money, heard all these things and sneered at him. And he said to them, 'You justify yourselves in the sight of others, but God knows your hearts; for what is of human esteem is an abomination in the sight of God.'" Lk 16, 14-15

"Then an argument broke out among them about which of them should be regarded as the greatest. He said to them, "The kings of the Gentiles lord it over them and those in authority over them are addressed as 'Benefactors'; but among you it shall not be so. Rather, let the greatest among you be as the youngest, and the leader as the servant. For who is greater: the one seated at the table or the one who serves? Is it not the one seated at table? I am among you as the one who serves." Lk 22, 24-27

"If there is any encouragement in Christ, any solace in love, any participation in the spirit, any compassion and mercy, complete my joy by being of the same mind, with the same love, united in heart, thinking one thing. Do nothing out of selfishness or out of vain glory; rather, humbly regard others as more important than yourselves, each looking out not for his own interest, but [also] everyone for those of others." Philippians 2, 1-4

"Not many of you should become teachers, my brothers, for you realize that we will be judged more strictly, for we all fall short in many respects. If anyone does not fall short in speech, he is a perfect man, able to bridle his whole body also. If we put bits into the mouths of horses to make them obey us, we also guide their whole bodies. It is the same with ships: even though they are so large and driven by fierce winds, they are steered by a very small rudder wherever the pilot's inclination wishes. In the same way the tongue is a small member and yet has great pretensions. Consider how small a fire can set a huge forest ablaze. The tongue is also a fire. It exists among our members as a world of malice, defiling the whole body and setting the entire course of our lives on fire, itself set on fire by Gehenna. For every kind of beast and bird, of reptile and sea creature, can be tamed and has been tamed by the human species, but no human being can tame the tongue. It is a restless evil, full of deadly poison. With it we bless the Lord and Father, and with it we curse human beings who are made in the likeness of God. From the same mouth come blessing and cursing. This need not be so, my brothers. Does a spring gush forth from the same opening both pure and brackish water? Can a fig tree, my brothers, produce olives, or a grape vine figs? Neither can salt water yield fresh. Who among you is wise and understanding? Let him show his works by a good life in the humility that comes from wisdom. But if you have bitter jealousy and selfish ambition in your hearts, do not boast and be false to the truth. Wisdom of this kind does not come down from above but is earthly, unspiritual, demonic. For where jealousy and selfish ambition exist, there is disorder and every foul practice. But the wisdom from above is first of all pure, then peaceable, gentle, compliant, full of mercy and good fruits, without inconstancy or insincerity. And the fruit of righteousness is sown in peace for those who cultivate peace." James 3, 1-18

I ask the Bishops within the United States of America, in particular, after considering these instructions and the warnings of Jesus, to recognize the error of their ways in issuing a statement that says that they and other priests can deny communion to persons in political life who attempt to come to terms with the strongest of emotions on both sides of the abortion controversy; who do not necessarily advocate abortion, but advocate rather that this is an issue too complex and too varied to be decided by religious fervor. When you state that someone who supports a woman's right to control her body and her pregnancy may be denied Communion in their parishes, you are in fact stating that you are equal to Christ, the judge of us all, and that is simply not true. Christ teaches that you Bishops, above all, must show compassion, humility and understanding. By your statement concerning "Catholics in Political Life," you have been blind to all of these requirements.

CHAPTER III:
WHAT CATHOLICS BELIEVE

In order to fully understand what we as Christians believe, one must read, study and reflect upon the Word of God as embodied in the New Testament. The New Testament must be compared to the Old Testament in order to understand the new covenant between God and His people, which has been established through Jesus Christ. For a quick study of what we believe, reference may be made to the Nicene Creed, which we still recite as a part of our worship of God in the celebration of the Eucharist, during Sunday Mass. Our profession of faith reads this way:

We believe in one God,
　　the Father, the Almighty,
　　maker of heaven and earth,
　　of all that is seen and unseen.
We believe in one Lord, Jesus Christ,
　　the only Son of God,
　　eternally begotten of the Father,

God from God, Light from Light,

true God from true God,

begotten, not made, one in Being with the Father.

Through him all things were made.

For us men and for our salvation

> *he came down from Heaven:*

By the power of the Holy Spirit

> *he was born of the Virgin Mary, and became Man.*

For our sake he was crucified under Pontius Pilate;

> *he suffered, died and was buried.*

> *On the third day He rose again*

> > *in fulfillment of the Scriptures;*

> *he ascended into heaven*

> > *and is seated at the right hand of the Father.*

He will come again in glory to judge the living

> *and the dead,*

> *and his kingdom will have no end.*

We believe in the Holy Spirit, the Lord,

> *the giver of life,*

> *who proceeds from the Father and the Son.*

> *With the Father and the Son he is worshipped*

> > *and glorified.*

He has spoken through the Prophets.

We believe in one holy, catholic

and apostolic Church.

We acknowledge one baptism for the forgiveness

of sins.

We look for the resurrection of the dead,

and the life of the world to come. Amen.

A further explanation of Catholic teaching is beyond the scope of this work. *The Catechism Of The Catholic Church*, published by Liguori Publications in 1994, even in small print size totals 803 pages and its companion, a total of 975 pages. The catechism is an instruction in our faith and addresses a host of issues, not the least of which are:

† Man's relationship to God

† How God reveals Himself

† Catholic heritage from the Apostles

† Christ as the "Word" of God

† Sacred scripture – the Old and New Testaments

†   How scripture speaks to our hearts through the guidance of the Holy Spirit

†   The Many Aspects and Significance of Faith

†   An in-depth analysis of the Creed

†   The Holy Trinity revealed

†   What we believe God to be

†   Creation and its mystery

†   Angels

†   The World as we see it

†   How we understand sin

†   The fallen angel – Satan

†   Jesus as God and as Man

†   Jesus – born to the Virgin Mary

†   Jesus crucified and risen

†   The last supper as part of Catholic worship

†   The Church's Apostolic Mission

†   Forgiveness through baptism

†   Resurrection to life and in body

†   Heaven and Hell

†   Judgment

†   Liturgy

✝   Sacramental Christian life

✝   Confession of sins

✝   Living Christ like

✝   The Importance of Morality

✝   Freedom of choice (good versus evil)

✝   Virtues (faith, hope, and charity)

✝   The Commandments

✝   Prayer

If you are not Catholic or not of some other Christian experience, you may not fully understand our Creed. For you, we Catholics believe:

That our Creator so loves us that He was willing to take our human yoke upon Himself, to feel in that form all that we feel, and ultimately to take upon Himself the task of providing the only penance equivalent to the insult which our sins cause our Creator, God the Father, a penance which was and still is the willing sacrifice of His life for the forgiveness of all of our sins.

That our Creator aspires for us to be equal in dignity to his Son, so that He can share Himself more fully with us throughout eternity. If He merely desired pets, His Spirit would not encourage us to grow in our potential and He would not have provided this existence by which we might learn to distinguish that which is essentially good for us from that which is essentially deleterious. A lesson which the fallen angel has yet to embrace.

That when God looks upon us, He wishes for us to be a reflection of His nature and not of our own. He has given to us a dignity, which we mistakenly but harmlessly refer to as human dignity. From this proceeds love, joy, respect, unselfishness, and moral conscience. It is for these reasons that we do not believe that scripture is intended to be the literal Word of God, interpreted without understanding the culture, history, or objectives of its human authors. God does not wish for us to merely be His lackeys, and nor did He desire this of those who actually wrote the words of the Bible. If God wanted it to be His literal words, He would have written it Himself; He hardly needed human authors to do it for Him. He meant for us to be guided, therefore, in its interpretation by Him (in this context by the Holy Spirit). In this way, the words can come alive for and be special to each one of us. They can mean something different each time we read them, but not be any less true, depending upon what we are searching for on that occasion. The Bible allows us to interpret it in light of our personal needs, failings, and the yearnings of a particular occasion. This is as God's words were meant to be. Alive and meaningful to us each time we read them.

That when we recite our Creed or the prayer known as the "Our Father," the word (men) means "men and women," and we believe that women are of no less stature than men, although Jesus' actions seemed to define different roles for men and women. In His choice of the first twelve apostles, Christ was also showing us the practicalities of that time in human history. Who, 2,000 years ago, would have followed a Messiah whose only disciples were women? Our maturity within the time table of human history teaches us that men and women are equal in the eyes of God, He who is not defined by sexual classification, but who nevertheless created both sexes.

That God, our God, is a rather impressive being (I Am Who Am), One who has the same freedom of choice which has been given to us, His creation, not some small God who can be bargained with or controlled by mere humans. So when "born-again Christians" state that, "Since I have accepted

Jesus Christ as my personal Savior, I am now saved," we Catholics give pause and reflect upon that portion of scripture which is not open to interpretation:

"For just as the Father has life in himself, so also he gave to his Son the possession of life in himself. And he gave him power to exercise judgment, because he is the Son of Man. Do not be amazed by this, because the hour is coming in which all who are in the tombs will hear his voice and will come out, those who have done good deeds to the resurrection of the life, but those who have done wicked deeds to the resurrection of condemnation. I cannot do anything on my own; I judge as I hear, and my judgment is just, because I do not seek my own will but the will of the one who sent me." Jn 5, 26-30

That it is wrong, against the will of God, for any Catholic, for any Christian, to hate his brother (in this sense, any other human being) simply for the sake of hate alone or for the maintenance of prejudice. Therefore it is wrong, and must be corrected, for whites to hate blacks, for blacks to hate whites, for the Irish in certain parts of this country, to hate anyone who isn't Irish, for Christians to hate Jews, for Jews to hate Christians, for Palestinians to hate Israelis, for Israelis to hate Palestinians, or for "claim-to-be-Christians" to hate Catholics. For it is our hate that defines us and, as we hate, so shall we be judged.

That we as Christians are the light of the world, for we have been called and we do proudly follow Jesus, the actual Light of the World. Many of us don't recognize that we are the light, or that being so carries with it certain responsibilities to the world. Some of us still follow the fearful God in the Old Testament without really understanding the full impact of the new Covenant or the joy to be found in the Good News. Some of us don't really understand what it means to be Catholic, because what it means at times just isn't easy. It isn't easy to pick up one's cross and carry it each day, day after day, in following Jesus Christ. We often falter along the way. Then, we begin again. It isn't easy at all.

That Mary, as the Mother of God, rightfully plays a special role in the Church, and like other sons who have a difficult time saying no to their mothers, that she can pray with us to her Son, Jesus, and help us obtain from Him what we truly need.

That selfishness and arrogance can be our undoing. We further believe that although we can't earn our salvation by doing good deeds, without good deeds, without putting words into action, the change of heart required for entrance into God's kingdom will not be present when the Day of Judgment for each of us comes; and it will come.

That we need to share what we have with others, to sacrifice for others, to help those less well off. We believe that government must reflect these values; that Medicare, Medicaid, Headstart and other social programs which help others should be paid for by our taxes. We believe that the most fortunate, who have benefited the most from a free society and free market economy, should carry the greater burden. We believe that the greed and avarice shown to us, time and time again, by large corporations, their CEOs and Directors, must be eliminated once and for all. There is no justification for the extreme disparity between wages paid to an executive of a company as compared to its office workers, mill workers or miners (with a possible exception for the person who spent most of his or her life building that particular company).

That the environment isn't just "the environment," an abstract term. It is our environment, our human habitat. Its condition determines whether we drink pure water or polluted water; breathe clean air or dirty air, whether we will lose our coast lines or instead retain our beaches; whether our plants and animals will grow healthier or die prematurely; whether we will need sunscreen in the future with an SPF of 15 or one of 2000; whether we all will have enough to eat in the future; and whether our food will nourish us or poison us. We believe that good stewardship is not only necessary to fund our parishes, but also to save our planet. Saying that there is no such thing as global warming, or giving it another name, doesn't make the problem go away. Shame on those who would rather ignore the problem in order to pass it on to the next generation, which generation may find that the same problems have grown to such a magnitude that no solution will present itself.

That our Catholic Christian faith separates us from those who seek pleasure over sacrifice, selfishness over good works, worldly treasure over heavenly treasure, status over equality, privilege over stewardship, arrogance over justice, and lies over truth.

CHAPTER IV:
THE CHALLENGE AND HOW IT MUST BE ANSWERED

A. THE CHALLENGE TO THE ORDAINED

The challenge for both the clergy and the laity is to stop insisting that change is bad. The Catholic approach to Christianity has traditionally recognized God's concern as well as respect for His creation. His love and respect for us are recognized in those gifts which He has given to us; the ability to discern right from wrong, the desire to be treated justly and to do the same to others, the ability to reason, to discover and to explore (to expand our knowledge of ourselves and our universe) and the ability to love others besides ourselves. Of these gifts, we Catholics have always held the gift of reason close to our hearts. We recognize the importance of the gift and the expectation of God that we will use it. Two examples of this tradition come to mind; the first is expressed by way of story and the second from *The St. Joseph Edition of The New American Bible*. The first is the story about the devoutly religious man whose house was overcome by floodwater. As a result, he had to climb out of a second floor window and get up on the roof top. A rescue boat came by and offered to take him to safety. He refused, stating that God will save me. Later, a helicopter came by and its crew offered to take him to safety. He refused, stating that God will save me. Eventually, the flood waters encompassed his entire house and the man drowned. When he woke up he was in the presence of God. He asked, "God, why didn't you save me"? God responded, "Why didn't you take either the boat or the helicopter which I sent for you?"

The preface to *The Saint Joseph Edition of The New American Bible*, entitled "Dogmatic Constitution on Divine Revelation" states in part: "—since God speaks in Sacred Scripture through men in human fashion, the interpreter of Sacred Scripture, in order to see clearly what God wanted to communicate to us, should carefully investigate what meaning the sacred writers really intended, and what God wanted to manifest by means of their words. To search out the intention of the sacred writers, attention should be given, among other things to "literary forms." For the truth is set forth and expressed differently in texts which are variously historical, prophetic, poetic, or of other forms of discourse."[4]

How would biblical scholars know this, but for the gift of reason? How are we to apply the Word of God, as expressed in the New Testament, when those words were written to address remarks and parables spoken by Jesus over two thousand years ago; before we understood that homosexuality is not a matter of choice and that soon we will have to contend with nanobots, robots which are too small to be seen with the naked eye, and can be breathed into the lungs and then move on up to the brain without the person even knowing it. But for God's gift to His creation of the ability to reason, we would be little different than the animals of the field.

What are we to reason about the Church to which God has called us through his Son, Jesus Christ? Perhaps that the Vatican financial scandal, clergy child abuse, homosexual and heterosexual priests who dismiss their vows of celibacy, cover-ups within the Church and other mistakes will only be repeated in the future unless we demand another way. Why should the laity, who have been baptized in the Holy Spirit and been reinvigorated with the Holy Spirit through confirmation, be excluded from leadership? Do they not reason? Can they not discern right from wrong? What is the clergy afraid of? Loss of Power? If the current course of the

Church hierarchy is not an issue of maintenance of power, then there is no reason not to share power with the laity.

B. HOW THE ORDAINED MUST HELP

When someone comes to you, whether you are the Pastor or Associate Pastor, Monsignor, Bishop or Cardinal, or even Pope, with something to say, even if it appears on the surface to be a complaint, don't out of hand dismiss what that person is saying, just because they are angry; either with you, with previous ways in which things have been done, or with some other person or policy within the Church. Listen for the Word of God. We are taught that we are a temple of God and that the Holy Spirit dwells within us. If that is true, you need to be less dismissive of what we have to say. This requires that you see through our pain and determine if there is any validity to our suggestions or criticisms. If in good faith you ascertain that something should be changed, and that change does not interfere with or in anyway undermine the teachings of Christ, then you have an obligation to God and to his people to affirmatively act to implement that change.

HOW IMPORTANT YOUR HOMILY IS!

I have met quite a number of Priests who take the

position that they are neither there to entertain nor to inspire the congregation by their homilies. To you I say, get another job, the priesthood does not become you. You've forgotten your way and there maybe no way back from your own personal crisis.

Our priests have to remember that while they are attending to the Lord's chores all week, we have been working for a living, caring for our children or elderly parents, trying to make time for spouse, working overtime, watching the news (and being informed of murders, rapes, child molestations and wars), attending meetings, traveling, encountering every sort of difficult person or difficult circumstance, lending an ear, or making a handout, sharing in a friend's loss, or helping a stranger, and your Sunday homily is your only opportunity this entire week to lift us up, to fill us with joy, to encourage us, to instruct us, to admonish us, and to challenge us. It is, however, never your opportunity nor your prerogative to bore us.

We have come to know and understand that the Word of God was intended to be a spoken word. Show us by your example and by your words how we are to give effect to God's Word in our lives, families, and businesses. If you are not comfortable or confident in doing this, then find someone who is. The Holy Spirit has touched deacons and lay parishioners alike. Allow those who feel compelled to share his teachings, to share and teach in your place, if you are not a confident speaker. You can review and approve in advance what is to be said that Sunday, but have the courage to step aside when you are not the best equipped or the best prepared to inspire. It is a greater failing to disappoint your parishioners and to condition them to dread your homilies, then it is to allow someone else more gifted than you to raise them up. As it is said in Scripture, each of us is given different talents. Don't be offended or consider your calling diminished if enlivening the Word of God is not one of yours.

You must use introspection to your advantage and allow it to help you grow into the type of priest which Christ wants you to be. Look at your shortcomings and failings as well as your strengths. Seek help from those who can strengthen within you what needs strengthening. Make friends among the laity. Ask them to share with you their talents and together your deficiencies or limitations can be reduced or eliminated. Seek professional help from psychiatrists, psychologists and counselors when needed. If those selected by the Church within these categories are ineffective, seek out the same professionals within your community. The power of prayer is a powerful blessing. Pray often and ask others to pray for you. Do not be afraid to admit your weaknesses. Very few, if any of us, can successfully traverse this maze, which we call life, without turning to someone else, admitting our failings, and asking for help to overcome them. We do this every time we walk into a confessional, and priests are no exception.

Do not, except most briefly, shield yourselves with the defense mechanisms associated with pride or arrogance. Borrowing a slogan from the United States military, we need you "to be all that you can be" for I would hazard an educated guess, that given an opportunity in a survey about their parishes, 4 out of 5 Catholics would indicate that they or someone in their parish has been offended in one manner or another by their Pastor or by another Catholic priest. You have no idea what damage you do when you lack the patience or genuine interest to listen, with understanding, to what someone else is trying to say to you. If your immediate reaction is to raise the defense mechanisms in order to come up with a quick response to what you are hearing, your response is likely to be ill-considered and misguided. The number of parishioners whom you have turned away from the Church by your conduct is staggering. I have a difficult time coming to grips just with the number which I alone have encountered. I even encountered one in the weeks prior to concluding this book when I was looking for a commercial artist. I contacted one and explained to him the concept behind this book and what I was looking for in the way of art work for it. Before I could finish the description, he interrupted and posed the following question; "Are you Catholic or are you Christian?" My response, of course, was that they are one and the same. His reply was, "No, they are not." I then found myself being lectured by a now born-again Christian, a misinterpretational literalist, spouting John Chapter 3, Verse 3 at me. Fortunately, I had my first experience with a born-again Christian approximately two decades ago, and then went in search of the answers to their questions. Unfortunately, this person was what I would label as the typical born-again Christian, who has all of the answers, is unwilling to be guided by the Spirit, and who will not be contradicted. They, and only they, know the mind of God and the rest of us, Catholics, Methodists, Lutherans,

Presbyterians, and other main line Christian denominations are all from the devil and are damned. If, as a member of the Catholic clergy, you are not concerned about creating more of these, then continue to do what you are doing now. Alienate us, fail to admit you don't know everything, don't pursue humility, and don't offer understanding, forgiveness, and peace.

As members of the clergy, you need to reach out to us, to your parishioners, those who are called the laity. You need to accept the fact that we too have been touched and can be touched by the Word. Reach out to us and we will reach back. Welcome us into positions of leadership and we will accept the challenge. Treat us as equals and you will be blessed with our talents. Fear us, object to us, attempt to humiliate us, continue to disenfranchise us, and as hard as we try to turn the other cheek, we will likely respond in kind. You see, our human failings are very much the same as yours. Help us to be all that we can be. For those who have left, invite them back into the Church. For those of us within the Church who feel ignored, recognize us. We need to work together to get our house in order so that we can invite all other Christians back into the Church, the Church which Christ intended for all Christians.

Originally, I had decided not to share with you, my readers, any of my personal experiences, for fear that my detractors would use these for the purpose of excusing the importance of the challenges presented by this book. On the other hand, it is important for everyone to understand that the issues presented in this book are not conjured up from my imagination, but instead come to me from my experience and the experience of others. I trust then that you will understand how difficult it is for me to relate even one of those experiences.

Some years ago, I truly felt a calling to become involved in stewardship within my parish. I felt very strongly that I was being led to this calling. At a meeting of approximately twelve members of our parish council, the diocesan director of stewardship turned to me and said "I am not really sure what it is, but I think you should be the first chairman of this parish's stewardship committee." At that time, as a member of the parish council, I was very motivated to do whatever I could for our parish community. It was also during this period that we had a Pastor who was not well regarded as a leader, but surprisingly enough had a gift for choosing men and women of talent for service on the parish council. I therefore found myself within a group of brilliant and committed lay people. Unfortunately, it was also the failing of this Pastor to never take the work of the parish council and see it through to the point of completion. After several years, most of us on the parish council were frustrated and disillusioned. It was the same Pastor who refused to make stewardship an essential element of the day to day work within the parish. Members of the clergy might be inclined to say that this pastor and they, are human, and as humans they are going to make mistakes. Yes, that is true, but you need to stop making the very big mistakes which are evident in the Church's recent history. You must understand that if your behavior is not Christ-like, you will push us away from Christ, away from the Holy Spirit, or away from the Church.

How can the ordained help? Invite us into positions of leadership. Share authority over the governance of the Church. Trust that we too know what is good and what is evil, as well as what is best for the Church and what is not best for the Church. Allow us to lighten your load, to reduce your burdens, and to more fully participate in our Church.

Letter from a Parishioner to his Pastor

Father _____
St. _____ Church
His address
His City and State

Dear Father _____ :

Today is Ash Wednesday, the first Ash Wednesday that I can ever remember having no interest in going to church or in getting ashes. There has also never been a time that I can remember being so angry for so long. The way you handled the Parish Council meeting on _____, has been described by those who have called me after the meeting as shocking, insulting, and embarrassing. I share their views.

Even if someone is lacking management skills and has had no training in interpersonal relations, it would have been basic common courtesy for you to have contacted _____, _____ and myself prior to that meeting to let us know that you were going to immediately and unilaterally institute a two-year term for members of the Parish Council and immediately dismiss those who had served at least two years. It would have also been basic common courtesy, even if you didn't mean it, to thank the people who you would be dismissing from the Council, for their service, considering the fact that they are volunteers who take time away from their families to help the parish.

Parishioners have told me stories for years about how you have alienated other parishioners and how those parishioners have then gone to other Catholic churches in the area. It was easy for me to dismiss those stories as exaggerations until the same type of behavior was directed at me. If the parishioners who are committed volunteers and church leaders are treated this way, then I can just imagine how the average parishioner feels about St. _____ Church.

There are certain critical behaviors or elements which must be part of any organization's character if that

organization is going to be successful. In the case of St. ____
__ Church, members of the parish (1) must feel appreciated;
(2) must feel as though there is accountability; (3) must
have good two-way communication; and (4) must feel that
their clergy, paid staff, and church leadership cares about
them (good public relations). In the way you handled the
dismissal of Parish Council members, you failed to show
any gratitude, you embarrassed the members whom you
were dismissing (evidencing a complete failure of good
public relations), and you failed to communicate to those
members beforehand your intentions, thereby allowing
them to be "set up," embarrassed, and "cut off at the knees"
at the meeting.

In terms of accountability, you should have embraced
the Parish Council's inquiries about the Finance Committee
rather than becoming defensive about them and allowed the
Parish Council to suggest to you that a Finance Committee
that only meets at most twice a year to put together a budget
(or perhaps to rubber stamp a budget already prepared
by the parish office) is not the type of finance committee
that provides oversight and accountability to a parish.
Without accountability, you can never expect stewardship
to succeed at St. _____. In the vast majority of parishes
nowadays, parish administrators are being utilized to
enhance accountability, and yet at the last meeting you
firmly rejected that notion, stating that we would have to
wait 17 months when your replacement would take over as
pastor of St. _____, before a parish administrator could be
selected. We can't sit idly by for the next 17 months.

With the exception of where I needed to call the ushers'
coordinator, I am going to give you examples of my own
experience, rather than the experiences of other parish
members. You insulted me and showed a complete lack of
respect for the time that it took me to prepare (as all ministry
heads were requested to do) a handout for their respective
ministries for Ministries Weekend. I prepared a handout
for the Parish Council doing nothing more than describing
issues that we had at one time discussed or had scheduled
on an agenda to discuss in the future. Rather than calling
me to discuss any revisions, it is my understanding that you
simply vetoed the handout, and neither you nor anyone in

the parish office showed me the courtesy of getting back to me to let me know that we weren't going to be using it for Ministries Weekend. I had to find this out myself on Ministries Weekend when the Parish Council had no handouts at their table. Once again, breach of fundamental organizational principles (total lack of communication), which caused the volunteer to be frustrated, aggravated, and to feel unappreciated.

This past weekend when the parish newsletter was to be handed out at all of the masses between the end of communion and the final blessing, I find that this was not done at all of the Masses. Rather than jumping to the conclusion that you again ignored what was supposed to have been done, I contacted Mrs. _____ and asked if she or her husband received any instructions from the parish office. The message she received was that it was to be handed out at all masses but she received no specific instructions as to when during the mass or in what manner. She also volunteered that she often received messages from the parish office late on Friday, and she has often had difficulty receiving timely messages or seeking further explanation when necessary, because by the time that she gets through picking up her children from school and her other responsibilities, the parish office is closed. She will sometimes get a message that simply says to call the parish office for further instruction. If she receives such a message late in the day on a Friday, she has no way of finding out what the message is except to call the emergency number on the weekend and ask that you call her. She indicates that she has specifically asked ____ to leave ____ home phone number so she can follow up with _____ if necessary, and apparently _____ refuses to do so. I cite this simply as another example of lack of communication and lack of good public relations.

As members of the church leadership, how can we express to others that they should commit their time, talent and treasure to St. _____ and represent to them that they will be appreciated for doing so, when we ourselves are not appreciated for doing so?

I have taken the time to put this in a letter to you, because prior to this time I did not think I could be civil to *you if we met in person. Many people have offended me in my lifetime, but never have I been so strongly offended by a Catholic priest, let along the pastor and leader of my parish.*

One of the individuals who called me one or two days after the Parish Council meeting, who had only heard what had happened, recommended that I stay on at St. _____ regardless of how embarrassed or insulted I might have felt, suggested that I wasn't the only person that you so substantially insulted in such a fashion in recent times, and thought this might be your attempt to stir up the creation of a delegation from St. _____ to go down to see the Bishop and insist upon your retirement. If this is your intention, it would certainly be a lot easier if you simply came to us and asked us for our assistance in approaching the Bishop to convince him to allow you take your retirement immediately.

No one on the Parish Council who has sought change through observation, comment, or even criticism has done so out of malice, but only with the best interests of the entire parish in mind. We have attempted to be frank and forthright with you and if you were offended by our forthrightness, then you had an obligation to inform us of how you felt.

My initial reaction was to do what many others have done before me; give up on St. _____ and go elsewhere. Upon further reflection, I have decided that it would not be in the best interest of the future of St. _____. I have seen too many people go to other parishes, and I observe at almost all of the masses, substantially reduced attendance over the last year. I do not wish to allow St. _____ to continue to stagnate. On the other hand, in order to accomplish any of my work at St. _____, I will need the cooperation of each member of the clergy and of all parish employees.

I hope that you will look upon this as an opportunity for healing, and for the re-establishment of our relationship (where I felt as though I could tell you anything without you becoming defensive). I would like to speak further with you about this, but will leave it to you as to whether you wish to do so (by whether you call my office to schedule an appointment for me to meet with you at your office or for you to come here).

Very Truly Yours,

Writer's Identity Protected

Postscript: I'm told by this parishioner, now several years later, that he never received a response to this letter nor was he contacted by this priest; a missed opportunity for reconciliation.

C. THE CHALLENGE TO THE FAITHFUL– BIBLE, PRAYER, COMMITMENT, AND PARTICIPATION

Catholics who haven't learned to participate in the liturgy must now do so. We are called to worship God together as a community. We can't do that if we don't verbalize the liturgical responses or join in singing the hymns. If you can't sing, at least follow along by verbalizing the words. Over time you'll become comfortable enough that you know the words and how they are to be sung that you will be able to join in. Not unlike life itself, you can only get out of it what you put in. Observers of life never experience life.

Observers of Christ never experience Christ. As Catholic adults, far too many of us rely upon our attendance at Mass each week, the few scriptural readings from the Old and New Testaments read aloud during that service, and the teaching that the priest brings through his homily, as our primary, or sometimes sole source, of spiritual maintenance. Such is all too understandable in our increasingly complex and frenzied world. However, acceptance of this routine without any further sacrifice, will never lead us closer to God. Until we read and study the Bible in its entirety and pray regularly for ourselves, our friends, our relatives, our communities, and those whom we have injured or who have injured us, we will never grow into what Christ wants us to become. He wants us to become a greater reflection of Himself. When He looks at us, He wants to see more of Himself. Make no mistake, this does require commitment and sacrifice. We must set aside the time each day to do so, and that is what makes the commitment so difficult.

Someone once said that life happens while we are waiting for life to begin. If your first realization occurs just prior to your death that you really haven't led the type of life which your Savior desired for you, your last moments on earth are going to be extremely difficult. We can only hope then that the Church's conception of purgatory, a place that we can first go after death to be cleansed of any remaining sins, does exist, and will in fact be available to us. Nevertheless, we need to prepare ourselves daily, for we know not when our time will come.

The people of Christ within the Catholic Church can no longer continue as spectators. When I attempted to establish a Stewardship Committee within my parish, the request was made to a parish of approximately 3,600 families for volunteers, approximately 8 or 9 came out to the first meeting and only 5 or 6 remained active on a regular basis. Our parishes cannot continue to be operated only by the few who are willing to make a commitment. That commitment must be made by all of us as an acknowledgement of our membership responsibilities. As a member of Christ's Church, we must contribute as much of our time, God-given talents, and finances as we can, of course not overextending ourselves nor making ourselves either physically or psychologically ill as a result. Our parishes operate and function properly primarily due to the good will of their parishioners. If for a certain duration, you lack the available time to make a commitment, then perhaps consider increasing your monetary contributions to the parish. If you're strapped for cash, but have some free time that you can invade and can sacrifice for the good of your parish, then by all means become involved in one or more ministries. If you feel as though due to illness or other limitations, you cannot contribute either, then please take the time each day to pray that someone may take your place and that they will be blessed for their sacrifice.

Understand too, that the parish community, its Pastor and staff, and all of its buildings and facilities are not simply being provided to you by the Bishop of your diocese or by the Pope in Rome. Our parishes exist and only continue because we, the parish members, voluntarily contribute the funds necessary, the $1,000,000 to $2,000,000 which it takes to run the average parish. Depending upon the financial needs of your particular parish, the absolute minimum to be given by any one family, barring economic difficulty is probably somewhere in the range of $8.00 to $15.00 per week. For those of you who give one dollar or less in the collection basket each week, you really need to perform an examination of conscience. Start by asking yourselves: "Out of my income and resources, is a return to God through his Church on earth of $52.00 per year, adequate, to thank Him for all the good things He has given to me?"

Tithing, is not just a concept mentioned in the New and Old Testaments, it is a requirement of membership in the Body of Christ. If the Church has failed to make this clear to us, then let us be clear from this point forward. I would like to share with you an excerpt from the first "Education in Stewardship Newsletter," which I authored for my parish approximately seven years ago.

"In examining the principles of Catholic stewardship, the hope arose among the members of the parish council that St. _____ could become a stewardship parish, and this hope was shared by our pastor. Why did the parish council feel strongly that stewardship should become the foundation for the future of our parish? This turns upon what stewardship is, and to arrive at that, perhaps we should look at what stewardship is not. It is not simply another fund raising drive. It is not the giving of time, treasure and talent because it's the "in" thing to do.

When Jesus came into the world, He had a very important message for each one of us, which we often don't really understand. The message was that sacrifice was to be the essence of our Christian lives. Jesus taught us this by his own example when he gave his life in sacrifice for our sins. It is much reflected in the gospels of Matthew, Mark, Luke and John, that Christ, in addition to the ultimate sacrifice of his human life, sacrificed often by way of fasting and prayer. The giving of our time, talents and treasure can take the place of fasting (although fasting can and should periodically be an appropriate sacrifice) but nothing can take the place of prayer, so as a good steward, WE MUST REMEMBER TO ALWAYS PRAY FAITHFULLY AND REGULARLY.

Much of Christ's teachings are not only difficult for us to understand but are also many times difficult for us to hear. For example, St. Luke relates to us Christ's rules of charity in his gospel (Luke 6:27-36) in which our Lord states "But I say to you who are listening: Love your enemies, do good to those who hate you. Bless those who curse you, pray for those who calumniate you. And to him who strikes thee on one cheek, offer the other also; and from him who takes away thy cloak, do not withhold thy tunic either. Give to everyone who asks of thee, and from him who takes away thy goods, ask no return. And even as you wish men to do to you, so also do you to them. And if you love those who love you, what merit have you? For even sinners love those who love them. And if you do good to those who do good to you, what merit have you? For even sinners do that. And if you lend to those from whom you hope to receive in return, what merit have you? For even sinners lend to sinners that they may get back as much in return. But love your enemies, and do good, and lend, not hoping for any reward, and your reward shall be great, and you shall be children of the Most High ..." [This scriptural passage was from an earlier edition of *The St. Joseph Holy Bible*].

If there is anything that Christ's stay on earth taught us, it is that being a Christian is not intended to be easy; that much is expected of us, but that also much is our reward in return, both here on earth and also in the kingdom to come. Stewardship, then, is the carrying into action of the original call of Christ to us, to follow Him. We need only mirror ourselves upon the face of Christ and ask if He were a plumber, or an electrician, a school teacher, a nurse, a doctor, lawyer, accountant, seamstress or retired pensioner, would he become selfish, look after his own needs only, and neglect the needs of others. How, then, can we do differently and still say that we follow Christ and that we are truly Christians?

Stewardship, then, is the opposite of selfishness. It is the selfless act of sacrificing some portion of our income and wealth (accumulated assets) in support of (1) our Church in which we claim membership, and (2) charities that help the poor as well as other worthwhile causes. We sometimes foolishly think that what we earn and what we have accumulated is solely due to our own efforts, and yet, if we had not been blessed with good health or with the courage to overcome infirmities, we would never have earned or accumulated anything. If God is equally responsible for what we are able to earn and accumulate, then what does He expect in return?

Many people would respond by indicating that God doesn't need money, which is true. This, however, overlooks the fact that God's people, and the world provided to us by God, does require money in order to pay for food, clothing, health care and shelter. Our own church pays interest and principal on the loan that was taken out in order to construct the all-purpose building in which we have our Masses, other services, and various functions. Our Pastor is required to pay salaries for parish staff; for utilities; insurance; building maintenance; and the list goes on. When we make a contribution to the Church then, we are helping to pay the expenses of the parish community, and our contributions will also assist in supporting our various ministries and services to our parishioners.

For some, conscience will dictate that they return to their church fifty percent, or forty percent, or thirty percent of what they earn annually, or of the wealth that they have accumulated. For many of us, we may feel comfortable being guided by the scriptural recommendation that we at least tithe (SIR 35:8-9; Matt 23:23). A tithe is generally defined to be ten percent of one's gross income. As an example, if someone were to contribute ten percent of his or her annual income, by giving five percent to St. _____ and five percent to other charities, and that person were earning $36,400 per year, his or her weekly contributions in the offertory would be $35.00 each Sunday. Our parish presently falls woefully short of even a ten percent stewardship commitment (five percent to the Church and five percent to other worthy charities.)

We believe that in large part, the Church itself is to blame for this through its failure to educate us on our responsibilities as followers of Christ. In looking at stewardship, the parish council has come across the terms "joyful giving" and "joyful giver", and when one realizes that there is joy in giving, the value of stewardship is then understood. Stewardship or sacrificial giving is food for the soul, and the more that we can nourish the soul, the more that we can strengthen our relationship with our Creator, the better prepared we will be for the time when we will meet our Creator and be required to give an accounting of ourselves. Perhaps if we could, as Catholics, fear God less and realize more of God's love for us, we would be able to see that sacrificial giving is a way of opening and offering our hearts to Jesus."

CHAPTER V:
A PLAN OF ACTION

A. RESPONSIBLE LEADERSHIP

The Catholic Church has failed miserably in its attempt to govern itself from the top down and to the exclusion of its lay members. An all male, sexually repressed and frequently non-celibate clergy has proven itself unfit to lead Christ's Church. The term "Catholic" by definition means universal. For the Church to be truly "Catholic" it must admit the unordained to leadership positions. The current all male, all uncaring, all unsympathetic, all unaccountable, all capricious leadership must go if the Church is ever to be renewed through its members, who themselves are not without spiritual guidance.

The laity must become shareholders in Christ's Church. Their participation must no longer be limited to merely reporting to those priests who have appointed them. Until the laity occupy positions of authority, perhaps even eventually equivalent to those held by the Cardinals, accountability and trust between the ordained and the Body of Christ will never be re-established. Lay leadership should be welcomed rather than feared; embraced by the clergy, rather than spurned; because it opens up a nearly unlimited supply of human as well as financial resources. Do you among the clergy believe that your disappointing collections, which are even worse now after the celibacy scandal, could not become even more strained if you refuse to hear what those around you are trying so desperately to tell you?

There are only two reasons why the ordained in positions of authority would refuse this marvelous opportunity to involve the laity in their own Church. The first is to maintain their positions of power, no matter the cost; and the second reason is to refuse the call of the Holy Spirit, for the entire Body of Christ is led by the same spirit; the same eminence; one that does not speak only to the ordained. To refuse to hear us, is to refuse to hear your own conscience. To refuse to hear us is to refuse Him who has sent us. Come judgment day, what could possibly be your excuse?

If forty years ago, or longer, we were on governing boards within the Church to which complaints of child abuse and other breaches of celibacy were made, we would not have covered them up. We would not have reassigned the offenders to different parishes, unsupervised or even unannounced, to commit criminal and unacceptable acts against their parishioners and against their children. We would not have protected our positions by secret settlements, which are now not so secret, rather than addressing the cause of the problems. We would have admitted our inability to deal with the situation, rather than try to save face, if we could not have more appropriately handled it. You have abused our trust and destroyed our confidence. Admit your failings and extend your arms and hands to us. Bring us from the fringes into the core of the Church. We can help you. You only need allow us to do so.

We can bring a perspective to the Church which those within it do not have, and cannot possibly possess. For within the hierarchy you are self-absorbed; you cannot see the forest from the trees; your objective is to maintain the status quo, rather than adjust to the needs of those whom you claim to serve. This is a lonely world; a cruel world; a vicious world; one which it is impossible or nearly impossible to travel alone. Very few are capable of living a celibate life. It must no longer be mandatory. For those few who can attain it in all of its purity, they should be commended. But even for them, it should be aspirational. The celibacy debate has raged for centuries. It is time to stop debating it. It is nearly impossible to overcome the strongest of all human emotions, the human sex drive. We have been pre-designed and pre-engineered as sexual beings; not something that we can merely wish away. Priests who would be better priests if married should be allowed to marry, rather than be forced out of the priesthood. Those who have been forced out because of marriage should be welcomed back. There is no valid reason for these men to be punished any longer. Our God is not a jealous God. He would welcome happier, healthier, family-oriented priests. He is willing to share Himself with them and their families.

On the other hand, if you can maintain your vow of celibacy, commit yourself solely to Christ, and to his Church, then you should do so. If you are convinced that your calling can be bettered by a solitary commitment to God and the Body of Christ, undiluted by the responsibilities inherent in a relationship with a spouse or children, then all of the power of God and our prayers and support shall be with you. May God bless you and keep you with Him all of the days of your life. But don't claim that yours is the only way. Welcome those who wish to partner with both God and another human being.

B. HOW MIGHT LEADERSHIP BE SHARED

One model for shared leadership would begin with parish councils being fully elected by the laity, and comprised of between six to twelve members, depending upon the size of the parish. The first step would be to establish an electoral committee to oversee the process. The first electoral committee could begin with the heads of all of the parish ministries. The first electoral committee might continue for two or three successive terms, during which it would establish procedures by which volunteers from the parish could be nominated and then voted upon. The members of the parish council would serve for two year terms, with any members seeking re-election being challengeable by another parish member. There would be no term limits so long as the parish consents to a member's re-election. The parish council would be responsible for hiring and for the termination of the parish's administrator. The parish council and the parish administrator would be responsible for all further hiring, budgeting, contracting, and operations for the parish, freeing up the Pastor to concentrate on his liturgical, sacramental, teaching, and counseling duties.

Each diocese would have a diocesan counsel, with each parish represented by one member on that council. The diocesan council would be responsible for diocesan-wide planning, budgeting, real estate acquisitions, staffing, and for requests from individual parish councils for the re-assignment of clergy. It would also act as the appellate body to hear and decide appeals of all of the Bishop's administrative decisions, from the type and design of new churches or expansions to complaints and concerns from all staff, clergy and non-clergy alike.

All meetings and conferences of the Bishop, or of all Bishops within a particular country, would be open to and represented by the diocese's Bishop and one lay member from the diocesan council. Equal contributions to the agenda, committee assignments and speaking opportunities would be accorded to clergy and non-clergy alike at these meetings and conferences. Ultimately, this democratization of the Church could be extended further, if the Body of Christ so desires.

C. ADULT EDUCATION

The world around us is moving more swiftly than any one of us, even a decade ago, could have imagined. The vast majority of us are working more and enjoying it less. The unseen battle between God and his fallen angel rages around us, within us, and against us. We do not fully understand why our lives have become overwhelmingly difficult. We look to the Church for answers and there are few to guide us. A Sunday homily leaves us cold as if once a week was sufficient anyhow. We are pulled at by the secular world as if being laid siege to. We have a need for the Church to lead us and to expand our spiritual horizons. We desire to understand our place in this world and what God expects from us. We need our clergy to seize each opportunity to shepherd us and to understand the importance of not wasting even one homily; of structuring their homilies to relate to our every day lives; and finding others to render those homilies if they themselves lack the ability to enliven the Word of God.

The Church must break from routine and urge its adult parishioners, or perhaps even require them, to continue their religious education throughout their lives. If requiring adults to attend classes or workshops is not initially practical, then perhaps the Masses need to be rescheduled to allow for additional teaching time during them. Begin by educating us on the importance of continuing adult education and how a seven to ten minute homily, once a week, is just not sufficient to refresh our souls or impart knowledge to us on how stewardship and charitable acts are the opposite of selfishness and how selfishness itself may perhaps be the greatest of all sins. Educate us on our duties and responsibilities to one another, and unlike certain Christians, teach us that our place is not to shun one another, nor judge one another, but to encourage one another to do what is right. For very few of us don't know what that is; or if we don't know, it is because we have hardened our hearts throughout our lives by our own decisions.

In sales and marketing, there is a concept best described in these words "attitude determines altitude." One's perspective, if positive, can significantly increase one's chances of successfully soaring to the height necessary to achieve one's objectives in life. To put it another way, attitude is everything. It is the duty of the clergy to help us understand that calling ourselves Christians and actually acting as Christians may be two entirely different things. Help us to understand that viewing attendance at Mass as an obligation is different from viewing attendance at Mass as essential to the purpose of giving thanks to God. Help us to distinguish more clearly between the God of the Old Testament and the promise of the God of the New. Educate us as to why we should not fear death, or if we do, what changes we must make in our lives and in our attitudes, so that we no longer fear death.

I once heard Father Bob Hunt speak at one of his engagements within our parish with respect to attitude. He suggested that perhaps one of the most favored theories within the Church on judgment, was one in which we might actually be given the privilege by Christ to judge ourselves. According to this concept, we receive opportunities each day in our lives to say either "yes" to God or "no" to God; perhaps in whether we formally welcome a stranger, say hello to a neighbor, or in how we respond to a request from someone for help. It becomes a matter of how we treat those closest to us and those furthest from us. How we apply the commandments or respond to Christ's teachings "everyday of our lives." If we mostly say "no", if we look at our glass as half empty rather than half full, we will develop a certain lifelong attitude, from which it may be impossible to deviate, then when asked by Christ at our time of judgment, "Do you love Me," we may instinctively reply with the wrong answer, if we have fostered the wrong attitudes. In this regard, it becomes incumbent upon those of you who are in our clergy, to continuously educate us; to remind us and continue to remind us, to cajole us, to make us think, and to teach us to be introspective. Please don't waste any opportunity, any moment to do so, let alone the time reserved after the reading of the gospels, the period of time which we refer to as "the homily."

Teach us to be introspective. Lead us in an understanding of what is perhaps the greatest failing of men and women around the word, Catholics and non-Catholics alike, that so few of us are introspective. In whatever position we take or whatever beliefs we pursue we are just so absolutely right, and that is what is wrong. How can we be right about everything? We are all imperfect human beings who should be using the life given to us to struggle towards perfection. The time when we think that we know it all, is the very time when we should become more introspective.

Introspection must become as regular of an activity as is our morning or evening prayers, attendance at Mass, or our sacrifices for others. Introspection takes the time to question ourselves and challenge our self-contained belief that we are right and others are wrong. We need to ask ourselves questions like, did I treat that person fairly, patiently, respectfully, with understanding, and with humility? We need to ask ourselves if another person feels so strongly about something in such an opposite way as to how we feel, are we certain that we are right and they are wrong. Does that other person make a compelling argument? Does that other person's position make sense? Should we perhaps embrace a different position? We need to understand that changing our minds about things, that searching for a greater truth, is not a weakness, but is a strength, and should be commended. We are generally hardest on our politicians and elected representatives when they change their positions. Rather than being so, we should look at the new position and determine whether it is better than the old. If so, we should commend those people for having open minds and the willingness to search for the greater truth or the better solution.

Very few Catholics embrace the Sacrament of Penance through confession.   I fully understand this because of how embarrassing and how extremely difficult it is to bear our souls and to convey our sinfulness to another mere imperfect mortal. It is however, a difficult necessity. We all know how important it is to get something off of our chest, meaning that it helps the healing process to speak to someone else about what bothers us. We often utilize a best friend for day-to-day frustrations, and sometimes we seek help from a professional, be that person a psychiatrist, psychologist, or counselor. Our approach to confession is one of introspection. We begin with an examination of conscience. If we don't reflect upon how we have sinned against God and sinned against our brethren (other men and women), we can hardly avoid the near occasion of sin nor grow in a spirituality which will keep us from sin. There is one particular pamphlet concerning the examination of conscience entitled, "Speak Lord...your servant listens," distributed by the Marians of The Immaculate Conception, Marian Helpers, Stockbridge, Massachusetts, 01263, which can be ordered by telephoning 1-800-462-7426 and asking for pamphlet BR5. I recommend that all Catholics utilize this publication or a similar one as a guide in making a good, honest, and truly healing confession. I invite all Catholics to renew themselves through the spiritual healing which is available through this Sacrament of Penance.

D. ACCOUNTABILITY

Accountability requires more than simply saying that one is accountable, more than just distributing an annual fiscal report, and more than just telling parishioners about how their contributions have been expended. It requires permanent safeguards that cannot be interfered with or changed from one Pastor to the next and requires the active participation of the laity. You must ask us what we need and what we desire. If funding is not available to continue all programs, you need to ask us which programs we are willing to sacrifice. Alternatively, you need to ask us whether we are willing to come up with any additional funding to keep the existing programs. Please stop making these decisions without us.

Accountability means responsiveness to parishioners' concerns and complaints. A change in Pastors in our church, for example, led to the removal of suggestion boxes. By his actions, what message has that Pastor sent to us? The inference was that he simply didn't want our suggestions. If there was some other reason, such as the continued blasphemous action of dropping a communion wafer into the box, perhaps that reason needs to be given to us, and should be given to us not just once, but over several months so that even those who were sick or on vacation will be privy to the message at least once. Accountability means explaining your actions when there is little time to consult with us on what we think is best or appropriate. Take the opportunity to explain to us the need for a change in priorities or why a decision we have approved has not or cannot be implemented. Accountability means trusting us as partners in our joint pursuit of salvation through Christ Jesus.

E. THE CHURCH AS A RESPONSIBLE ENTERPRISE

The Church needs to be a responsible enterprise, similar to a business, in order to understand the importance of keeping its books in balance, keeping its customers (its parishioners) satisfied, and in being cognizant of the importance of properly marketing itself throughout the world. Within the Church, we need to approach our parishioners and those who might join the Church as we would in marketing the products or services of any business. We need to train those in positions of contact, the staff in the parish office or rectory, and the heads of our ministries, in the ways of civility, encouragement, hope, and charity. We must use every opportunity to reinforce in those who contact us that they are important, valued, and respected. In other words, we need to market our parishes both to our parishioners and to those who might become parishioners. Good first impressions as well as satisfied subsequent impressions, can go a long way to enhancing participation, contributions, and trust. This would be in keeping with the sentiments expressed in a plaque my wife has kept since she was in high school which reads, "Kindness in words creates confidence, kindness in thinking creates profoundness, kindness in giving creates love."

CHAPTER VI:
THE NEED TO AVOID DIVISION

A. WITHIN THE CHURCH

As I conclude the writing of this book, I have been practicing law now for nearly twenty-five years. During much of that time I have centered my practice in the areas of elder law, trusts and estate planning. Many good people have placed their trust in me because of active participation in their church community and I truly appreciate their confidence. Many have shared with me their concerns about the Church and their frustrations. I all too well understand their anger when they make suggestions to a Pastor and those suggestions are ignored. I have served on many a parish council and seen unanimous agreement of the lay members inappropriately or unnecessarily disregarded by the person in whom the Church vests authority within the parish, the Pastor. He then wonders why his collections can never reach above a certain level. Within the Church, whether we realize it or not, the only vote accorded to us is the amount of almighty dollars which we place into the collection basket.

If ignored, we can bring the organized Church to its knees. We, Christ's disciples and followers, "the Body of Christ," would still continue the Church, but in a different fashion, which might, for all we know, be evolutionarily pleasing to God. However, not knowing the mind of God, we must first endeavor to ask our ordained brethren to hear our cries for change and ask them in good conscience to no longer ignore our pleas.

LET ME MAKE THIS AS CLEAR AS I POSSIBLY CAN, I AM NOT ADVOCATING AT THIS TIME THAT WE WITHHOLD CONTRIBUTIONS FROM OUR PARISHES FOR THOSE CONTRIBUTIONS ARE ITS LIFE BLOOD AND SHOULD CONTINUE EVEN IF WE DISAGREE WITH HOW WE ARE TREATED BY THE CHURCH HIERARCHY. The difficulty here is that our Church has been in existence now for over two thousand years and tends not to change very quickly. On the other hand, priests and laity together have been calling for changes for over four hundred years, ever since the time of Martin Luther and the Protestant Reformation. For that reason alone, the changes called for should come quickly. I am not sure that any of us has the patience to wait it out even another decade without substantial change.

The challenge then for the ordained and unordained alike is to quickly come together in order to recognize the strengths and benefits to the Church of increased lay participation and increased lay authority. If the ordained cling to their positions of power and authority and continue to ignore those of us who constitute the Body of Christ on earth, it will be their selfishness, their self-centered objective of maintaining their positions which will create the greatest division within the Church since the time of Martin Luther. The clergy must understand that we can no longer be ignored, displaced or in any way told to leave the Church. We are the Church. We would like to continue to think of the Church as clergy and laity working together to do Christ's work on earth. The challenge then is as we extend our arms and hands to our ordained brethren whether they will accept us as equals, with varying talents, a source of strength and commitment to be embraced, rather than feared. If it takes fear to be heard, rather than reason, then let our resolve strike fear in the hearts of those whose primary interest is preserving their own authority rather than seeing to the work of our Lord. Customs may simply need to change.

I am imploring those of you currently within the Church

hierarchy to heed this call and to not force Christ's people from his Church. The last thing we really need is anymore division within the Church. We don't need anymore separatists establishing their own "Catholic" churches. Those who believe that the Mass must be spoken in a foreign tongue, "in Latin for example," within an English speaking country, are just plain wrong. Of the many positive reforms of Vatican II, is our ability now to understand, more clearly, our own words of worship and, as a result, we better understand the reasons why we worship and why we do certain things within the Mass.

The Church has wisely seen the need for change and has positively responded in the latter part of the last century. It now needs to recognize that change is not always bad and that the change which is now being requested is simply long overdue. The Catholic Challenge then is a call to all of us to work together to improve participation within the Church, to increase adult education and the meaningfulness of our faith, and together to strengthen our Church by drawing upon the talents of each of us. May God bless us in this endeavor and hold us close to His heart.

B. BETWEEN CATHOLICS AND OTHER CHRISTIANS

As the Church from whence you came, we do look for unity with other Christians and hope and pray that you will sometime within the near future rejoin the Church. Perhaps if we as Catholics extend to ourselves more of the right of self-governance, we would be in a better position to welcome those of you back to us who already experience and value this right. In the meantime, be guided by the Holy Spirit and follow your conscience. If you believe that you have a strong and meaningful relationship with Christ and your worship of Him is well directed, then know as Catholics that we are with you and we support you in the difficult struggle it is to live life as a Christian. For those of you who have already heard the call of the Holy Spirit and are now in the process of converting to Catholicism or who have already done so, you may already be experiencing the rewards of your faith. Many people convert to Catholicism for a number of different reasons. There is a feeling of comfort in the fact that the teachings of Christ within the Church have not changed for over 2000 years. On the other hand, administrative directives and non-dogmatic changes have occurred, continue to occur and must occur, for the Church to be a living and breathing representation of Christ on earth. Consequently, the Church's position on the need for celibacy can change without being seen as a retreat from Christ's teachings.

A woman in my own parish, who had been a devout Jew all of her life, awoke one morning and felt that she was simply called by the Holy Spirit to come into Christ's Church and she converted many years ago. Some of the notables who have converted to Catholicism in recent years include United States Senator Sam Brownback; the well known entertainer and comedian Bob Hope; former U.S. Solicitor General and 1987 United States Supreme Court Judicial nominee, Robert Bork; the Reverend Leonard Klein who had been a prominent Lutheran Pastor for 30 years and a former editor of *The Lutheran Forum*; and Mark Belnick, a former devout Jew and former General Counsel of Tyco International Ltd., who was acquitted of any wrong doing in Tyco's financial collapse; and certainly many others whose news of conversion has simply not reached my desk. Let's also remember that praying for unity is a wonderful thing but for unity to ever occur, we are the ones who must make it happen. We are not all expected to join monasteries or become cloistered nuns. We are, however, expected to use the abilities and talents that God has given to us. One need only reflect upon the message contained within any number of the gospels.

"It will be as when a man who was going on a journey called in his servants and entrusted his possessions to them. To one he gave five talents; to another, two; to a third, one-- to each according to his ability. Then he went away. Immediately the one who received five talents went and traded with them, and made another five. Likewise, the one who received two made another two. But the man who received one went off and dug a hole in the ground and buried his master's money. After a long time the master of those servants came back and settled accounts with them. The one who had received five talents came forward bringing the additional five. He said, 'Master, you gave me five talents. See, I have made five more.' His master said to him, 'Well done, my good and faithful servant. Since you were faithful in small matters, I will give you great responsibilities. Come, share your master's joy.' {Then} the one who had received two talents also came forward and said, 'Master, you gave me two talents. See, I have made two more.' His master said to him, 'Well done, my good and faithful servant. Since you were faithful in small matters, I will give you great responsibilities. Come, share your master's joy.' Then the one who had received the one talent came forward and said, 'Master, I knew you were a demanding person, harvesting where you did not plant and gathering where you did not scatter; so out of fear I went off and buried your talent in the ground. Here it is back.' His master said to him in reply, 'You wicked, lazy servant! So you knew that I harvest where I did not plant and gather where I did not scatter? Should you not then have put my money in the bank so that I could have gotten it back with interest on my return? Now then! Take the talent from him and give it to the one with ten. For to everyone who has, more will be given and he will grow rich; but from the one who has not, even what he has will be taken away. And throw this useless servant into the darkness outside, where there will be wailing and grinding of teeth." Mt 25, 14-30

"The lamp of the body is the eye. If your eye is sound, your whole body will be filled with light; but if your eye is bad, your whole body will be in darkness. And if the light in you is darkness, how great will the darkness be." Mt 6, 22-23

"No one who lights a lamp hides it away or places it [under a bushel basket], but on a lamp stand so that those who enter might see the light. The lamp of the body is your eye. When your eye is sound, then your whole body is filled with light, but when it is bad, then your body is in darkness. Take care, then, that the light in you not become darkness. If your whole body is full of light, and no part of it is in darkness, then it will be as full of light as a lamp illuminating you with its brightness." Lk 11, 33-36

"The tax collectors and sinners were all drawing near to listen to him, but the Pharisees and scribes began to complain, saying, "This man welcomes sinners and eats with them." So to them he addressed this parable. "What man among you having a hundred sheep and losing one of them would not leave the ninety-nine in the desert and go after the lost one until he finds it? And when he does find it, he sets it on his shoulders with great joy and, upon his arrival home, he calls together his friends and neighbors and says to them, 'Rejoice with me because I have found my lost sheep.' I tell you, in just the same way there will be more joy in heaven over one sinner who repents than over ninety-nine righteous people who have no need of repentance." Lk 15, 1-7

"I am the true vine, and my Father is the vine grower. He takes away every branch in me that does not bear fruit, and everyone that does he prunes so that it bears more fruit. You are already pruned because of the word that I spoke to you. Remain in me, as I remain in you. Just as a branch cannot bear fruit on its own unless it remains on the vine, so neither can you unless you remain in me. I am the vine, you are the branches. Whoever remains in me and I in him will bear much fruit, because without me you can do nothing. Anyone who does not remain in me will be thrown out like a branch and wither; people will gather them and throw them into a fire and they will be burned. If you remain in me and my words remain in you, ask for whatever you want and it will be done for you. By this is my Father glorified, that you bear much fruit and become my disciples. As the Father loves me, so I also love you. Remain in my love. If you keep my commandments, you will remain in my love, just as I have kept my Father's commandments and remain in his love." Jn 15, 1-10

"Thomas, called Didymus, one of the Twelve, was not with them when Jesus came. So the other disciples said to him, "We have seen the Lord." But he said to them, "Unless I see the mark of the nails in his hands and put my finger into the nailmarks and put my hand into his side, I will not believe. Now a week later his disciples were again inside and Thomas was with them. Jesus came, although the doors were locked, and stood in their midst and said, "Peace be with you." Then he said to Thomas, "Put your finger here and see my hands, and bring your hand and put it into my side, and do not be unbelieving, but believe." Thomas answered and said to him, "My Lord and my God!" Jesus said to him, "Have you come to believe because you have seen me? Blessed are those who have not seen and have believed." Jn 20, 24-29

"When they had finished breakfast, Jesus said to Simon Peter, "Simon, son of John, do you love me more than these?" He said to him, "Yes, Lord, you know that I love you." He said to him, "Feed my lambs." He then said to him a second time, "Simon, son of John, do you love me?" He said to him, "Yes, Lord, you know that I love you." He said to him, "Tend my sheep." He said to him the third time, "Simon, son of John, do you love me?" Peter was distressed that he had said to him a third time, "Do you love me" and he said to him, "Lord, you know everything; you know that I love you." [Jesus] said to him, "Feed my sheep. Amen, amen, I say to you, when you were younger, you used to dress yourself and go where you wanted; but when you grow old, you will stretch out your hands, and someone else will dress you and lead you where you do not want to go." He said this signifying by what kind of death he would glorify God. And when he had said this, he said to him, "Follow me." Jn 21, 15-19

CHAPTER VII:
STEWARDSHIP

It is said that "money is the root of all evil." Is money the real problem, or is it rather the lengths to which we will go in order to obtain it and our apparent inability to part with it once we have it. The Ten Commandments, delivered by God through Moses tells us what we should do and what we should not do. Perhaps it is possible to sum them up in one rule "do not be selfish." There may be no greater sin that that which comes from elevating one's own desires over the needs of others. It is not so much cleanliness that is next to godliness, as it is unselfishness. When Christ and his apostles were walking through the wheat field eating grain, all that the non-Christians of that time could see were men eating without first washing their hands. This was of little importance compared to what he really wanted his apostles to learn. What did Jesus, through his ministry tell his disciples, "the first among you must be the last – don't seek to be at my right hand but to serve others." Stewardship then is not merely God's suggestion to us of our responsibility to give back something of that which

He has given to us, but His desire that we heartily embrace something, which by its very nature, will draw us closer to Him. In progressing through this life, we grow stronger in our faith and closer to God when we realize that stewardship is not just an obligation, but that it is at the same time spiritually rewarding. There is a certain satisfaction in knowing that one's monetary contributions have helped preserve the environment, protected an unwed mother or provided food and medicine for those who previously had none.

Stewardship in the Church means recognizing that everything good which we have comes from God. It only seems to us that we "earned it." Could we have earned it if we were blind, deaf, without either hands or feet? A few of us probably could succeed with one or more of these deficiencies. The vast majority, however, would be devastated. In almost all human suffering, a person who feels despair can usually find someone else whose condition is even worse. For what can we be thankful? Besides the air which we breathe, and the food which we eat, the inexplicable sacrifice of Jesus Christ for our sins, that we might have eternal life after this limited one. When you attend Mass or even at home gaze upon the crucifix, you see a crucified Christ. What a truly amazing love story. A God who so loved His creation that He would lower himself to the insults of human existence and make amends for us to God, His Father.

It was once explained in this way by a priest in one of his talks. If you or I insult another, that level of insult does not rise to the same level as where insult is made to the leader of a nation, since insult is not just to the one then, but to all whom that leader represents. When we insult (sin against) God, it is an infinite insult, which can only be satisfied by an infinite sacrifice, a sacrifice that only Jesus, being God, could offer on our behalf to His Father.

Stewardship then is a step forward in our faith by which we recognize and accept our obligation to support God's Church on earth as well as those who, for one reason or another, are not able to sufficiently take care of themselves. The Church refers to stewardship as an offering of our time, talent, and treasure to the Church and to others. In recent years, the Church has emphasized the need for stewardship, but has failed to bring its people to the level of understanding necessary for stewardship to succeed. For stewardship is not another way of raising money for church projects, but is an awareness of one's connection to the Creator. Without this, stewardship is a difficult concept to sell. It then sounds more like a pitch for buying one's way into heaven, which is just not possible.

Stewardship in the Church should not be a new nor a revisited concept. It should have been taught as part of our faith for the last two thousand years. If it had, the Church (and its parishes) would have more money than God (if you'll forgive the pun). Let's look at an average Catholic parish of say 3000 families. Let's also assume that receipts equal expenses and that it costs $1 million per year to pay for all of the staff, the upkeep of the rectory, electricity, water, sewer, insurance and the like. Three thousand families giving $10.00 per week in the offertory collection amounts to over $1.5 million in receipts for the year. Although ten dollars per week doesn't seem like much to give back to God, some give more than that and many give substantially less. When someone puts one dollar into the collection basket, and feels justified, is it really that person's fault, if the Church has failed to educate that person as to the scriptural basis for tithing, the needs of the Church as a physical institution, or the shallowness of his or her faith.

You don't have to like your pastor in order to contribute substantially to your parish (although it helps).

Parishioners need to be treated with respect and this can only be satisfied by the requisite accountability. What is required is that parishioners receive the assurance that the money is going to satisfy the needs of the Church and not line the pockets of anyone not entitled to it. Accountability means an independent auditor, not the pastor's golf buddy. Until the laity control the money or at least the manner in which accountability is ensured, the Church will never have the respect of its people (for anything other than Christ's own sacrifice). The ordained are fairly warned when we tell them "deal us in" or "deal yourselves out." Empower us and embrace us, and the Church will grow. Disregard us and disrespect us and the Church will die. For we are the Church, and you the ordained are to be its trusted stewards. The funny thing about trust though is that you have to earn it.

Stewardship cannot wait any longer. It must be engaged universally, in each parish, at the same time and with the same message. As the first Director of Stewardship in my own parish, I would like to suggest one model, there are many. The concept of stewardship should be introduced in each parish within a diocese, on the same consecutive six Sundays. It requires a thorough and complete introduction, and its themes must thereafter be repeated at least monthly.

After Hurricane Charley was predicted to hit the Tampa Bay area of Florida and at the last moment veered away, the Diocese of St. Petersburg took up a collection for Hurricane victims at all churches within the diocese. I happened to be attending Mass at one of the wealthier parishes the following weekend when the Pastor proudly announced that his church had collected $25,000 for relief purposes. I wish I could have gotten up and told his parish that I disagreed with their Pastor, that this amount was simply pathetic. This particular parish boasts over 4,500 registered families. Families who still have a roof over their heads, air conditioning (when it is 93°F outside and 80% humidity), jobs that haven't been displaced, electricity, food and water. This blessing was on average worth to them less than $6.00 per household. Shame on them and shame on all of us who don't understand what it means to sacrifice (for the benefit of others).

It is just as pathetic that Catholic parishes receive the vast majority of their financial support from only twenty (20) percent of their parishioners; at least that was the figure which we came up with when I served on the parish council at my church some years ago. I'm told now by a priest friend of mine, that the national figure is thought to be around thirty-two (32) percent. For this discussion, let's work with this figure. Does this mean that say sixty-eight (68) percent of our parishioners give a dollar or less in each Sunday's collection basket? I believe that it does. All you need to do is look around you at Mass during the offering. How many of those almighty single dollar bills are placed in the collection basket. Don't you think, as we all do, about those parishioners? One solitary dollar; that's the value of their relationship with God. How sad? Or is it?

The Catholic Church in recent decades, has from time to time, encouraged its parishes to begin stewardship programs. However, they are neither uniform nor universal. They fail more times then they succeed. There are three primary reasons for this. First, Pastors don't weave stewardship often enough into their Sunday messages (homilies). Second, the Church has never truly taught us that stewardship is really a part of our faith or a responsibility of membership.[5] Thirdly, far too many parishes have not been adequately accountable to their parishioners. Accountability comes in many forms but each form amounts to the same thing. If you are an accountable priest, you don't break your vow of celibacy and you certainly don't molest your parishioners' children. You don't steal from your collections and you don't leave your parishioners guessing as to where the money, once collected, has been spent. If you resolve these problems and teach stewardship as an essential element of our faith, parishes will no longer have financial problems. If they do, it will only mean that you and they have been encouraged by the increased sacrificial giving and have added far too many programs and services too quickly. Nevertheless, my bet is that even these will succeed.

Priests need to be cordial but firm with their parishioners. If it costs $1.2 million to run your parish, and you have 3,000 registered families, each family needs to contribute $400 per year to the support of the Church or a minimum of $7.70 per week. Yes, there are some families for whom even this amount would be a burden. They need not make this sacrifice and may do so with a clear conscience. Yet, the vast majority of the sixty-eight (68) percent of whom I spoke earlier can certainly make this minimal sacrifice. This formula though, should in most parishes, be the floor, below which few parishioners should go. Yes, there will be more (at least twenty percent) who will tithe or partially tithe.

If you look at the law given by God to Moses, you will see that those Ten Commandments can be summed up into one which states, "You shall love your neighbor as yourself." This is the equivalent of the following command: "Be not selfish." For selfishness is the greatest of all sins or perhaps more fundamentally is the basis for all sins.

The First Commandment

"You shall love the Lord, your God, with all your heart, and with all your soul and with all your mind."

If we are selfish, we will not share ourselves even with our Creator. We will ignore Him (until it is too late), we will fail to be grateful, to worship Him, to give Him thanks, to talk to Him, to listen to Him; all as we exclusively pursue the worldly pleasures available to us.

The Second Commandment

"You shall not take the name of the Lord your God in vain."

Boy, is this a tough one and I mean that sincerely, for I say that it applies to far too many of us, including myself. We do this by calling upon the Lord or using His name selfishly in anger rather than only in prayer and with the respect which is due our Creator.

The Third Commandment

"Keep Holy the Lord's Day."

I have always struggled with this commandment. As an attorney, in private practice now for nearly a quarter of a century, I have had to work on many a Sunday (after going to Mass) just to keep my head above water and to prevent the suicidal stress which one of conscience suffers when he feels that he might not deliver the finished product (a last will, trust or contract) by the date on which it was promised. Am I being selfish if I do so for my own preservation? I think not. Should I find a better way so as to not appear selfish? Perhaps. I take some consolation in the Gospel of Mark Chapter 2, Verses 27 through 28, "The Sabbath was made for man, not man for the Sabbath; that is why the Son of Man is Lord even of the Sabbath." It is to be both a time for giving thanks to the Lord as well as to serve as a natural break from our earthly toils.

The Fourth Commandment

"Honor your father and your mother."

When I applied for admission to law school, nearly 28 years ago, I was counseled by my professors to apply to as many schools as possible, it then being very difficult to get in. I was accepted to 90% of the 12 or so schools to which I applied. One of those was in California, which had a great campus and terrific climate. I was still in New Jersey at the time and opted to attend law school in Florida, a three-hour drive from where my parents had retired to several years earlier. It certainly would be easier to visit them I felt, if I lived relatively nearby. It also would be precious time, as you never know who will go first or how long after retirement either will live. My father died about 9 years ago. He was more than just a good man, and I have every confidence that God has smiled favorably upon him. For the last five years, my wife and I have been the primary caregivers for my mother who turned 90 years of age in August of this year (2004). We kept Mom in her own home well passed the time when she should have moved into a 24-hour facility of some kind. We did this by putting out and supervising her medications and vitamins; taking her shopping and to the grocery stores;

taking her to church; taking her to doctor's appointments; picking up her prescriptions; and solving whatever problems arose (from fixing prescription errors to changing batteries in the remote control for her television). This would have been an impossible task, considering my professional schedule, but for the tireless and unconditional contribution of time by my wife, Karen, who also holds down a full-time (or more than full-time) position as a benefits consultant. Karen, thank you so very much for your unselfish assistance in the care of my mother.

Mom broke her hip last year and has been in and out of the hospital six times in twelve months with other problems. If you have ever cared for a loved one, you understand just how much time can be expended by visitations alone, when each stay in the hospital averages about one week. It tends to set the caregivers back in their own work and responsibilities to others. Yet it is important because active family members, reviewing hospital charts and doctors' orders can prevent or stop so many mistakes in treatment from happening. Unfortunately, our medical professionals, doctors and nurses, but perhaps especially nurses, are over-worked and underpaid, and it does have an effect upon the quality of healthcare.

I have not always honored my parents as I should. I remember growing up in Warren, New Jersey, then a small rural town in the Watchung Mountains. My father, who loved cabinetry and who made everything from altars to vestment closets for our little stone and mortar church, wanted me to spend time with him out in our garage, building cabinets. As a not entirely unselfish youngster, I instead preferred to play after school and on the weekends with my friends. I only now regret my conduct in which I elevated my desires over those of my father. It is difficult to understand selfishness as a child. If we don't understand it as an adult, we could be endangering our very souls.

The Fifth Commandment

"You shall not kill."

This seems like an obvious commandment. However, even the simplest of directives seem for us hard to follow. The "us" I refer to is not just Americans, but also Saudi's, Pakistani's, Israeli's and those Muslims of many nationalities who butcher the teachings of any true religion. There is no God anywhere who is going to promise his followers that they will today enter paradise if they blow themselves up or destroy others in the process. Murder for ideological or political gain, only achieves worldly objectives, not heavenly ones, and is murder just the same. It is the responsibility of the Church (presently through its current hierarchy) to apply continuous moral pressure to influence those clerics in the Muslim world, who preach violence for the purpose of elevating their own positions to ones of power and prestige among their people, to stop. This selfishness must be combated by every facility and resource of the Church, for until we stop the poisoning of young minds, we will not stop the formation of new terrorists. The world around us is changing too quickly and becoming too dangerous for the Church to continue to carry on business as usual. The clergy must accept the challenge that the complexities of our time cannot be dealt with alone; they must involve the laity who have also been blessed with many gifts; not the least of which is a passion for justice for all peoples.

The Sixth Commandment

"You shall not commit adultery."

If you do, then what have you done? You have elevated

(selfishly) your needs, desires and gratification over the damage and injury which you could do to the emotions and security of your spouse. Many sins would never be committed if we would first place ourselves in the position of the person against whom we would be sinning. Alternatively, picture Christ in the room with you. Ask yourself, if Jesus was physically present, would I do this (thing)?

The Seventh Commandment

"You shall not steal."

When someone takes something which does not belong to that person, he or she is very selfishly saying to the victim, I don't care how hard you had to work for this, what you had to sacrifice, or that you may now feel violated or less secure. My desire to have it is all that is important. Another example of selfish elevation of one's own desires over the rights and expectations of others.

The Eighth Commandment

"You shall not bear false witness against your neighbor." A discussion of this commandment is set forth in Chapter VIII entitled Catholic Social Conscience.

The Ninth and Tenth Commandments

"You shall not covet that which belongs to your neighbor"

These worldly desires are rarely addressed in homilies. They hit close to home, perhaps reflecting a knowledge gained by the priest in the confessional. Besides the Old and New Testament's irrefutable declaration that the devil does exist, it is the temptations which we experience in opposition to these two commandments which most clearly testify to his existence. When some of us were growing up there was a television series, "The Flip Wilson Show" named after its star, Flip Wilson. Mr. Wilson, a black performer, did a routine, often in drag, which was very clever. It involved a character, "Geraldine," who always blamed the devil for everything which she did wrong. The famous line, which always received laughter, was "the devil made me do it." It was funny, because at that time, we all knew that there was no devil; the devil having convinced us that this was so. I wish I could better remember how the story goes. It started at a time when the devil realized that he was losing the war between himself and God, the war between good and evil. Then it dawned on him, if he could convince people that he did not exist, he would also be able to convince them that there is no sin. If people believed this, the devil reasoned, they would break all of God's commandments and he would then win the war with God. The devil knew that he wouldn't be able to change people's beliefs overnight, so he devised a plan that would slowly but surely give to him the ultimate victory. He set out to convince people that little infractions and small deviations from the commandments were really no big deal. You know what, they believed it and the devil's plan began working. The more people compromised their principles, the more the devil drew them to him, whispering in their ears, "that's fine, no problem, you can do that without guilt." Eventually, the devil convinced all of the people that they were as good as God, of equal status, and that there was no reason why they couldn't make their own rules. You know what, they bought it. Thanks be to God that this is only a story. Well, perhaps it is only a story for some of God's people, for the others don't believe that they are any different than before, and for them the devil has won. He has talked them out of unselfish desires, made foreign to them the concept of introspection (they are convinced that they are never wrong), and now counts them among his flock. This too is where the danger lies in thinking that we know how God would want us to vote on the most difficult issues of abortion or democratization of the Church. We can never really know the mind of God. Should we then be so presumptuous as to state that he is aligned with one group against another or with one position in opposition to another? Surely, such is folly in the eyes of our Lord.

(continued on next page)

SAMPLE PARISH FINANCIAL REPORT
_____ CATHOLIC CHURCH
SOMEWHERE, FLORIDA
"The Bottom Line"
for the 12 month period ending June 30, 2004
Parish Mission Statement

_____ is a faith-filled community of Catholic Christian believers seeking to become ever more fully a people of God, sharing the mission of Jesus Christ. We are called together and empowered by the Spirit to make increasingly true and obvious our response to God's will manifested to us through Christ. In prayerful discernment, we deepen our faith by being heralds of the gospel message of Christ as we minister to one another within the parish community, the Diocese, and throughout the world.

Together we are:
- 4,840 registered households with over 14,125 individual members.
- 90+ Ministries and Organizations.
- 1,517 ministers and volunteers.

Together we reach out to:
- 486 students enrolled in _____ Catholic School: PK – 8th grades.
- 704 students enrolled in our evening Religious Education Program: K – 8th grades.
- 641 children and young adults in our Youth Ministries & other Youth Programs.
- 446 sick & homebound each month, in private homes, 1 hospital, 6 assisted living facilities, 6 nursing homes and 6 retirement centers.
- 1,500+ of our brothers & sisters each year in our local community with financial assistance, both directly from us and through our St. Vincent de Paul Society.

Together we made it possible for:
- 1,000+ weekday and weekend Eucharistic Liturgies as well as many other opportunities for communal & private prayer and adoration.
- 184 infants, children and adults to receive the Sacrament of Baptism.

- 462 to receive their First Communion, Penance and the Sacrament of Confirmation.
- 53 couples to be joined together in Holy Matrimony.
- 683 to receive the Sacrament of Anointing.
- 100 families to be supported in celebrating a Catholic Funeral Liturgy.
- 140 students at our sister Parish in Nicaragua to attend school at a temporary facility.
- A refugee family of four to move from Liberia into our local community.
- Our diocese of _____ to continue its local, national and international works of charity through our participation in the Bishops Annual Pastoral Appeal.

Provided by the Parish Finance Council...committed to "Accountability and Transparency"

Staff...... parishioners.....

(continued on next page)

_____ Catholic Church
Financial Activities
For the 12 Month Period Ending June 30, 2004

<u>Support & Revenue</u>
Offertory Collection $____
Special Collections, Donations, Bequest $____
Bishop's Annual Pastoral Appeal Collected $____
Our Journey In Faith $____
Youth Ministries & Sacramental Fees $____
Regular Savings Interest $____
Parish Life Social Activities $____
Gift Shop $____
Miscellaneous Income $____

Total Support & Revenues   **$____**

<u>Expenditures</u>
Salaries & Employee Benefits $____
School Subsidy:
    Catholic School $____
    Religious Education $____
One time Bldg Fund subsidy $____
    Other Catholic Schools $____
Insurance, Utilities, & Telephone $____
Repairs & Maintenance $____
Liturgical Supplies & Materials $____
Bishop's Annual Pastoral Appeal Payments $____
Our Journey In Faith $____
Special Collections For Diocese & Nicaragua $____
Rectory Expenses $____
Contributions to Local Community Charities $____
Youth Ministries & Sacramental Fees $____
Office Expenses, Advertising $____
Capital Improvements $____
Parish Life Social Activities $____
Gift Shop $____
Other Expenditures $____

Total Expenditures   **$____**

Excess Expenditures From Savings   **$____**

*The _____ deficit was made up by withdrawing funds from the Church Regular Savings Account. The Regular Savings Account started the Fiscal Year at $_____ and ended at $_____. A deficit of $_____ is also projected for the current Fiscal Year (2004-2005) which will further reduce our Regular Saving account. The Finance Council is developing an aggressive strategy to meet this challenge and published those steps in the Bulletin insert distributed June 6th. Let us all pray and the Holy Spirit, our patron, will guide our efforts, inspire in each of us a true sense of giving and lead us ever closer to Him.

(continued on next page)

_____ Catholic School
Financial Activities (Inc. Evening Rel Ed Program)
For the 12 Month Period Ending June 30, 2004.

Support & Revenues
    Tuition $____
    Fees $____
    Parish Support: School $____
    Religious Education $____
    One time Bldg Fund subsidy $____
    Food Sales $____
    Student Activities/Athletic Income $____
    Donations: Restricted $____
    Endowment: Unrestricted $____
    Home & School Association $____
    Fund Raisers: Super Bowl Tickets $____
    Other Income $____

    Total Support & Revenues $____

Expenditures
    Salaries & Employee Benefits $____
    Instructional Supplies/Textbooks $____
    Office Expenses $____
    Insurance, Utilities, Telephone $____
    Repairs & Maintenance $____
    Capital Improvements $____
    Food Cost $____
    Transportation/Field Trips $____
    Athletic Expenses $____
    Fund Raiser: Super Bowl $____
    Other Expenses $____
    Payment of Retained Collections to Bldg Fund $____

    Total Expenditures $____
    Deficit Deferred to 2004-2005 $____

_____ Catholic Church
Combined (Church & School) Balance Sheet
As of June 30, 2004

Assets
   Cash Balances
      Checking:
         Church $____
         School $____
      Regular Savings $____
      Our Journey in Faith $____
      Building Fund Savings $____
      School Endowment Account $____
      Petty Cash:
         Church $____
         School $____
   Total Cash Balances $____

Property, Plant & Equipment
School Bldg, Land & Furniture $____
Rectory, Land & Furniture $____
Convent $____
Church, Other Bldgs, Land, Furniture $____
Total Property, Plant & Equip $____

Total Assets   **$____**

Liabilities
   School Mortgage Payable $____
   B.A.P.A. 2003 Balance Due $____
   Advance Collections for Tuition & Fees $____
   Restricted Funds:
      Journey in Faith $____
      Poor Box Balance Sheet Account $____
      Nicaragua Mission $____
      Miscellaneous $____

Total Liabilities   **$____**
Parish Equity   **$____**

Total Liabilities & Equity   **$____**

CHAPTER VIII:
CATHOLIC SOCIAL CONSCIENCE

Isn't it more accurate to speak of Christian Social Conscience? Don't we understand the terms Catholic and Christian to mean the same thing, each beginning with and at the direction of Jesus, the Son of God? What then is a conscience? Is its basis, human or divine? Does it matter?

We may think of conscience as that ability to determine what is good and what is evil; which conduct toward our neighbor is right and which is wrong; or that inner voice which urges us to move in one direction rather than in another. When we take the wrong turn, isn't it our conscience which reminds us of our imperfect choice. This conscience of which we speak attempts to override certain negative attributes which constantly tug at us; unrestrained pride, judgmental conceit (the erroneous belief that we are right in our determinations, even though an equal number of souls are of a different opinion), arrogance, cruelty, prejudice (of all varieties), selfishness, self-centeredness, unconcern for the welfare of others (their opinions, their poverty, their difficulties, their pain), hatred, obstinance, dishonesty, self-aggrandizement, narrow-mindedness, disrespect, belittlement, and sadism.

Our conscience appears firmly rooted in the Ten Commandments which direct us to honor the one God, His name, the Sabbath, mother and father, and our neighbor in the requirements that we neither kill him, covet his spouse, bear false witness against him, desire his possessions or separate them from him. It is also rooted in humility, unselfishness, kindness, mercy, compassion, peace, understanding and love. As such, what then is social conscience? Is the very term social conscience, redundant? In a world which is growing more uncaring, more frustrating, more dangerous and more difficult, can social conscience make a difference? If it can make a difference, does it require action on our part? What action is then required and which is appropriate?

The appropriateness of one's individual conduct can be easily measured by one yard stick; would Jesus act in the way in which I propose to or if He were visually present to me at the moment of my action, would I still behave in the same manner? If Jesus was visually present to me in a motel room, would I commit adultery with the spouse of another person?

Would Jesus the messenger of the new covenant, the Light of the World, the member of the Holy Trinity sent to show us that God loves each one of us no matter our faults or our failings, would this Jesus murder a doctor who performs a medical procedure which terminates a pregnancy? If you think that He would, then you don't know my Jesus, the Jesus born of the Virgin Mary and announced to us by the Baptist. But you need to get to know Him. Read His words, pray to Him, ask His mother to pray for you, and ask those who have gone before us marked by the sign of faith, to introduce you. It is essential that you get to know Him if you desire to fully develop your social conscience. Christ was infuriated with those who thought they knew everything (in his time, the Pharisees and the Scribes), Mk 3, 20-30; 7, 1-23; Lk 11, 37-54; Lk 12, 1-3; Mt 12, 22-42; Mt 15, 1-20; Mt 23, 1-39; Jn 12, 42-43. He was also adamant that love for Him was to be shown in this way:

"This is my commandment: love one another as I love you. No one has greater love than this, to lay down one's life for one's friends. You are my friends if you do what I command you. I no longer call you slaves, because a slave does not know what his master is doing. I have called you friends, because I have told you everything I have heard from my Father. It was not you who chose me, but I who chose you and appointed you to go and bear fruit that will remain, so that whatever you ask the Father in my name he may give you. This I command you: love one another." Jn 15, 12-17

If Jesus is telling us to elevate the needs of others, the concerns of others over our own, what does that mean that we need to do in the context of social conscience? Does it involve sacrifice? If so, in what ways?

Sacrificing ourselves for others likely means: (1) giving of our time and attention to others who will benefit from it; (2) sharing the fruits of our labors with others in need (some form of tithing); (3) supporting movements which seek to preserve or expand upon the dignity of others; (4) respecting, rather than deriding another person's difference of opinion; (5) spending the time necessary to become an informed voter, not one merely shaped by the occasional negative sound bite; and (6) avoiding the temptation to be guided by one or two significant issues, when there are almost always a host of important issues, the resolution of which is more significant for people (society) as a whole, than those one or two very emotional issues.

In scripture there are many references to the "last shall be first." In the same way, let us examine the last two elements of social conscience which are akin to the notion of social responsibility. Social responsibility requires both voters and candidates standing for election to relate to each other in terms of the highest levels of honesty and integrity. In regard to the individual as a voter, this involves putting others first and looking beyond the one or two emotional issues to which we have attached ourselves, in order to determine what is best for the greater good of our community, whether that community be our home town, our country or the entire planet. As a voter, one must ask, do I possess sufficient knowledge on a particular ballot issue to overcome the moral requirements of my conscience that I not vote blindly, foolishly, or in opposition to the general welfare of my community? If we are honest with ourselves, we must refrain from voting for or against that which we do not fully understand.

My own experience with the latter occurred in the year 2000 General Elections. In Florida we had more proposed State Constitutional Amendments than should ever be presented to any electorate. While standing in line waiting for an available voting machine, I observed as many people ahead of me and behind me as I possible could. I was appalled by the number of people who were requesting sample ballots in order to review these constitutional amendments for the first time while in line. Without reading about them in the months preceding the election, or considering the strengths or weakness of their proponent's positions on them, there was no way that these people could make an informed decision. Did that stop them from voting? I suspect not. It appeared that it was more important for them to make a choice, no matter how bad it might be.

With respect to choosing between two candidates who are standing for election to the same office, it would be helpful to have a model, a point of reference, an analysis to be applied to the suitability of electing a particular man or woman to political office. In that analysis, the characteristics which we refer to as honesty and integrity become two of the most critical elements of our focus, together with any campaign pledges which were made pivotal to a candidate's election; in other words, not to be deviated from. Because of everything that has happened to change the world as we know it in the last three or four years, it is that period which should serve as a case study for the future.

During this period, the United States President has been George W. Bush. He is supported by many good people who are emotionally tied to his anti-abortion and anti-gay marriage platforms. These platforms can have a very deceptive appeal. However, if we believe that Christian Social Conscience means that we must look beyond enticing slogans for the greater good of ourselves and our neighbors, it is essential to examine what a particular candidate really stands for, not just what his or her "spin doctors" wish for us to believe. Since actions speak louder than words, and pre-election promises mean little or nothing, how does candidate George W. Bush really stack up? What has his Presidency brought us? Are we better off now than we were before he became President?

There were two pivotal elements of Mr. Bush's campaign platform which made him a viable candidate in 2000 and probably helped him to be elected President. Let us examine his Presidency in light of his pledges to return honesty and integrity to the White House and to bring with him a compassionate conservatism.

Integrity and Honesty in the White House

The professional responsibility guidelines published for many professions, not the least of which are those that relate to the legal and accounting professions, indicate that in representing someone else you are to avoid even the appearance of impropriety. This is a very high standard, but perhaps the only one which would safeguard Americans against too much political cronyism. Granted, that each new administration, whether it be Republican or Democratic, will have a tendency to appoint from among its own, so long as the appointees are qualified in their fields and will carry out the responsibility to act in the best interest of all Americans, there is usually no significant problem. A St. Petersburg Times newspaper editorial from September 13, 2003, looked at the implications of a report prepared for certain members of the House Government Reform Committee, which report examined appointments made to the Dietary Guidelines Advisory Committee, which helps to establish dietary guidelines for all of us. The findings of that report were also supported by research performed by the Center for Science in the Public Interest. According to the editorial: "Most of those committee members have uncomfortably close connections to the food, drug or dietary supplement industries, the center found." After identifying a number of individuals who, based upon past employment or relationships, would not likely be looking out for the best interests of Americans in general, the editorial concluded with these comments: "More is at stake here than protecting a particular industry's profit. Nutrition and public health information released by the Federal Government should be based on the best science available not on political influence. Otherwise, its very credibility would be undermined."[6]

Since most of us simply do not have the time to monitor all that goes on in Washington, we have to rely upon those individuals in certain fields whose job it is to know what is going on. In a letter addressed to both me and my wife, dated August 24, 2004, which also acknowledged receipt of a contribution, the Union of Concerned Scientists states, "One of our top priorities this year is our campaign to restore the non-partisan manner in which science has traditionally entered into policy making decisions. An investigative report we released in February documents a pattern of suppression and distortion of scientific findings by the Bush Administration across a broad range of public policy issues.

These activities have serious consequences for human health, public safety and the environment."[7]

Mr. Bush has told us all that we are the beneficiaries of two tax cuts. He wishes for us to understand that he has done us a favor. The normal procedure would be to cut taxes in an environment in which you are also cutting spending. No one seems willing to do that and so our government borrows money to pay for its spending, because the revenue generated by taxes is not sufficient to cover the outflow. Perhaps we can look at this another way. If our government spends $400 to $500 billion more than it takes in from the payment of taxes, then we run into a negative or deficit situation. Have you ever tried to spend a $1.40 for every dollar you have earned? If you have, then you probably turned to credit cards to do so. Eventually you have to pay it back, and when you have to pay it back it hurts; with interest rates on those cards sometimes as high as twenty-two percent. How much is it going to hurt when we have to pay back this extraordinarily large debt, which Mr. Bush's spin masters claim is inconsequential; yet which Alan Greenspan, Chairman of the Federal Reserve, calls a threat to the foundation of our economy?[8]

If you wanted to return honesty and integrity to the

White House and in doing so avoid even the appearance of impropriety, why would you award billions of dollars in contracts to a company called Halliburton, without allowing other companies to bid for those contracts, when your Vice President, Dick Cheney, was the former CEO of that company? The usual response is, "Well, Halliburton was the only qualified company out there to handle this huge undertaking." Really? How do you know this without bidding the contracts?

I feel compelled to address the Eighth Commandment, "You shall not bear false witness against your neighbor," in light of Mr. Bush or his supporters' attack ads, with respect to the Swift Boat issue. Let's assume for the moment that challenges to the award of military service medals should take place over thirty years later, rather than when they are being awarded. The real issue here is not the medals. For the sake of the argument, let's take them all away from Senator Kerry. The real issue here is that rather than not serving in a combat zone, say by joining the National Guard, Senator Kerry accepted the challenge and threat to his life, and went to Vietnam; George Bush didn't.

We should also be careful to review the pledge of a

candidate to honesty and integrity in the light of general stewardship principles. For example, we expect our elected representatives, in particular our President, to obtain for us the best bang for our buck, the best return on our tax dollars. Few will argue that helping senior citizens with the expenses of their medical prescriptions isn't a good thing. However, when the price tag of that program might exceed $500 billion and potentially place the financial stability of Medicare in crisis, I am not so sure that it is a good thing.[9] Legislation should not be enacted primarily to obtain a political advantage against one's opponents, and especially when the price tag is simply too high. As Americans, we pride ourselves on wanting the best of everything, but there must be limits, or our community as a whole will suffer. For those receiving this Medicare prescription drug benefit, your social responsibility is to make sure that it was not received at too high a price. Was the elimination of the language, which would have given our government the authority, on our behalf, to negotiate the best prices for drugs, and the total cost to our economy for this program, too high of a price to pay?[10] See Endnote [11] for one American citizen's view on what has happened in Washington.

In an article written by E. J. Dionne, Jr., who writes for the Washington Post Writers Group and whose column was carried in the *St. Petersburg Times* on November 26, 2003, he states in part: "The drug bill faced defeat by a two vote margin and the Republican leaders in the house held open a fifteen minute role call, "for an unprecedented two hours and fifty one minutes." He further states, "...eventually, two Republications were hammered into switching their votes."[12] Should such important legislation ever be obtained in this manner? The two Republican legislators, who were persuaded to change their votes, were members of a group who were extremely concerned about the unusually high cost of this legislation, the impact upon the Federal deficit, and the future strength of our economy. These were traditional Republicans attempting to carry on with one of the traditional values we associate with the Republican Party, and that is fiscal responsibility. Should their concerns have been overruled out of political expediency? These are the questions we should be asking ourselves.

Do we as United States citizens understand that the vast majority of claims made by Secretary of State Colin Powell in his February 5, 2003 address to the United Nations, on why was it was so essential at that time for us to go to war in Iraq, have proven to be non-existent.[13] If the criticisms of Mr. Bush and his administration, that they exerted far too much pressure upon members of the intelligence community to shape their opinions in such a way as to support a war in Iraq, are untrue, then how could every single substantial basis for going to war in that country prove to have been false? Are people supporting Mr. Bush reasonably asserting, in good conscience, that the only truth teller in the country is Mr. Bush, and everyone who leaves his administration or writes a book about their experiences or who are in any way critical of him, are liars? In accordance with self-introspection, is that perspective reasonable?

One of the primary grounds strenuously argued by Mr. Bush as an essential reason for invading Iraq was that it both possessed and was developing weapons of mass destruction. David Kay, the investigator who was hand-chosen by Mr. Bush himself to enter Iraq in search of this evidence, found no weapons of mass destruction.[14] Mr. Bush was asked by people both within this country as well as others from around the world, to continue the pressure upon Iraq to permit additional weapons inspections and additional intelligence surveillance. He single-mindedly refused each and every one of these requests. If you don't believe that Mr. Bush abused the powers of his office and invaded Iraq primarily to eliminate Saddam Hussein, who it is reported threatened to kill his father when his father was still President, then what made it so expedient and so necessary to go to war at that moment in time? Prior to that invasion, Mr. Bush convinced all of us, and I think rightly so, that it was in our national interest and because of immediate security concerns necessary to invade Afghanistan and remove a government which was providing aid and comfort to al-Qaeda. Once successful in Afghanistan, did Mr. Bush steward us well thereafter? It appears in a review of the history of this conflict, that he failed to consider the cost, as measured in the loss of American lives and in the phenomenal increase that was required in U.S. government deficit spending (borrowing); that he ignored the warnings of many intelligent and knowledgeable people across our country who, prior to invading Iraq, urged him to consider that the factious tribes and groups within Iraq have historically never been able to live together, so he could not possibly expect to be able to bring democracy there within one or two short years.[15]

In terms of the management of this particular war, we weren't suppose to have to borrow substantially all of the money to finance it, or certainly not incur as large of a deficit as we have, because Iraqi oil revenues were projected to help pay both our expenses and the cost of rebuilding that country. Isn't it odd that we don't hear much about the fact that due to sabotage and lack of security, only limited revenue has been received from Iraqi oil.[16] Is this poor planning on the part of our government, poor management, or just plain foolishness? Certainly, the military has requested that additional men and material be sent to Iraq. Instead, with the upcoming election, Mr. Bush has sent scores of our service men and women from other bases overseas home in the hopes that their pleasure with him will be translated into votes come November. Those, unfortunately, are not the ones he promised to bring home by now. He promised our men and women in the Armed Forces within Iraq that they would be home sooner, on earlier rotations, and they instead have been asked to stay longer and have had to suffer the consequences of living under siege. Very few of us as Americans understand what that means.

My wife and I live in the Tampa Bay area of Florida and have been under siege for the last six weeks as predictions, first that hurricane Charley would make a direct hit upon our area, then hurricane Frances, and then hurricane Ivan. When you live in constant fear of losing your home, or perhaps your life, you receive a tiny understanding of what our men and women are going through in Iraq. How many of our soldiers have been killed, one thousand, fifteen hundred, more than two thousand? I would hazard a guess, and of course it is only a guess, that the powers which be believed that they could get in and out of Iraq with less than 200 casualties. Why? Well, on May 1, 2003, when President Bush originally declared victory in Iraq, there were 114 casualties.[17]

Mr. Bush has made it no secret during his term in office that he desires to see the repeal of the Federal Estate Tax. He recommitted to this proposal early on in 2004.[18] Repeal of any tax might be a welcomed event, if there was another source of revenue with which to replace the one being repealed. Under the current Federal Estate Tax Program, each U.S. citizen taxpayer can pass up to $1.5 million, federal estate tax free, at death, and a husband and wife can combine their exemptions for a total of $3 million. This individual exemption is already scheduled for increases to occur over the next four to five years to a point when most individual estates under $3.5 million and most married couples under $7 million will no longer be subject to the Federal Estate Tax.[19] The Federal Estate Tax currently impacts fewer than 6% of all estates in this country and, of course, has the greatest impact upon the largest of estates. I once also felt that the estate tax was confiscatory since taxpayers had, prior to death, paid taxes on earned income and on capital gains. I have since come to view this particular tax as a small price to be paid by those within our country who have become extremely successful as a result of our free market economy and democratic society. Shouldn't those who have been rewarded the most by the benefits of citizenship in this country give some of what they accumulated over their lives back to the community whose very structure permitted them to obtain such vast wealth?

I remember reading an interview with the senior Bill Gates, father of the founder of Microsoft. As a stockholder in Microsoft, his son made him a very wealthy individual. Unlike others with great wealth, he indicated that those who receive more from our society should in turn give back more to society. As President of our country, as the primary steward of our nation, does Mr. Bush share this philosophy?

What does the slogan "compassionate conservatism" mean to certain groups of Americans. Perhaps we can infer what their feelings might be from some simple facts and how those facts have been conveniently ignored by Mr. Bush. According to the U.S. Census Bureau, September 30, 2002, 41.2 million Americans are without health insurance coverage.[20] That's not 41,000, nor 410,000, nor 4.1 million, but 41.2 million Americans.   On Friday, September 26, 2003, the U.S. Census Bureau reported that the number of Americans living in poverty increased (not decreased) by nearly 1.7 million and that household incomes declined for the third year in a row.[21] The U.S. Census Bureau estimated in 2003 that, in the prior year, about 12 million American families were "worried that they couldn't afford to buy food."[22]

Mr. Bush, his Vice President, Dick Cheney, and his Secretary of Defense, Donald Rumsfeld, told us after we invaded Afghanistan that we had two other exceptionally dangerous regimes in the world, each of which were pursuing weapons of mass destruction. The first, of course, was Iraq, and the second was and is still North Korea. At one point,

Secretary of Defense Rumsfeld indicated that we had the resources and the determination to eliminate both of these problems. These three individuals promised us that they would deal with the most desperate and most dangerous regimes first and then made every attempt to convince us that they meant Iraq, rather than North Korea. They also stated early on, that they would not negotiate with North Korea. The interesting fact here is that we are certain that North Korea is developing nuclear weapons and already has several,[23] but we did not invade North Korea. In the case of Iraq, we presumed that they were doing so based upon very very flimsy indications. Why the difference in treatment? Also, why isn't North Korea any longer an issue, and why have we also made an about-face and entered into negotiations with North Korea rather than dealing with the problem presented there directly? Did we pick the wrong country to invade? If North Korea invades South Korea or attacks that country, don't we have mutual defense treaties which require our immediate response, and wouldn't that response potentially require the use of nuclear weapons? So then, which country was the bigger problem and the greater threat to our national security?

By choosing to invade Iraq and commit resources there, analysts as well as news commentators assert that we have taken an entire country and turned it into a breeding ground for terrorists. How might we have done this? By failing to commit sufficient troops in the first place to secure the borders and keep the elements of al-Qaeda out, which we now know to have entered the country.[24] By failing to utilize the Iraqi army to maintain control rather than disbanding it. By failing to be prepared to provide Iraqi's who supported the invasion with adequate personal security once we got there. By not planning ahead to deal with the civil unrest, which followed the invasion.

According to Maureen Dowd, a *New York Times* columnist, "Since America began its occupation, Iraq has become the mecca for every angry, hate-crazed Arab extremist who wants to liberate the Middle East from the "despoiling grasp of the infidels." Increasing numbers of Saudi Arabian Islamists are crossing the border into Iraq, in preparation for a jihad, or holy war, against U.S. and U.K. forces, security and Islamist sources have warned," *The Financial Times* said on Tuesday, quoting a Saudi dissident who noted that Saudi authorities are concerned that "up to 3,000 Saudi men have gone "missing" in the Kingdom in two months."[25]

By ignoring the pleas of our NATO allies and others throughout the world to not invade Iraq without them and without first pursuing every diplomatic avenue, we have stubbornly and fool-heartedly isolated ourselves from their support, potentially crippled our own economy to finance the invasion (and subsequent occupation), and, very likely, created for ourselves a much larger threat. There were sound policy reasons for waiting until a true coalition could be formed before invading Iraq, not the least of which was being able to do the job right.

It was interesting to watch and listen to the CBS program *Face the Nation* on Sunday, September 19, 2004. The panel consisted of Senator John Kyl, Republican from Arizona, Senator Chuck Hagel, Republican from Nebraska who serves on the Foreign Relations Committee, Leo Hamilton, Vice Chairman of the 9/11 Commission, and Richard Holbrooke, former Ambassador to the U.N. and now a Senior Advisor to the Kerry-Edwards Campaign. These men were first shown a film clip from the week before in which President Bush was telling an audience about how well we are doing in Iraq, that we are making so much progress, and that elections will even be held there as early as January (2005). Three out of the four, as sensitively as possible and without actually calling Mr. Bush a liar, disagreed with his assessment of what is occurring over there. As a matter of fact, they felt that the situation was going to get worse before our elections in November and even worse after that. One of the panel members, or perhaps two, noted that you could have elections in Iraq in January, but if you could not provide security at a sufficient number of polling places, and few people could vote, of what validity would those elections be?

What about Mr. Bush's remarkable assertion that he has the right to determine who is and who is not an "enemy combatant." He calls the current war we are involved in around the world the "war on terrorism," yet he and his advisors have refused to acknowledge that they have prisoners of war in their possession, choosing instead to label them as enemy combatants, attempting to create an entirely different category of prisoners. What does this mean for our men and women serving in the armed services overseas? It means that a country, which has prided itself for over 200 years on being the light of the world, a country which protects human rights across the globe, a country which stands for truth, liberty and, above all, justice, is now going to arbitrarily decide which prisoners will be covered by the protections of the Geneva Convention and which ones will not. Not only does this serve as fruitful propaganda for al-Qaeda's recruiting efforts, but it also mindlessly puts our service men and women, wherever they serve throughout the world, in heightened danger, because it now gives their captives even more of a reason to treat them with the lack of the same protections which would otherwise be available under the Geneva Convention. Do we want our elected representatives, in particular, our President, placing our soldiers in harms way in the first place and then making political decisions in the second place which further endanger their lives? Perhaps you missed the news reports discussing how ill-equipped soldiers were when they were sent into Iraq. Many of them even lacked essential body armor which their parents had to purchase at their own expense and send over to Iraq in order to protect their children.[26]

Recently, Vice President Dick Cheney launched a profusely absurd attack upon the Democratic nominee for President, when he stated the equivalent of, "If John Kerry were President on 9/11, he would not even have considered the attacks against us as an act of war."[27] What is he talking about? Every American, regardless of race, creed, wealth, poverty, or other social status, felt the same dread and the same horror on that date, an agony which Mr. Bush and Mr. Cheney are claiming was only felt by them. What kind of people make claims that they are so much better than the rest of us? Who would ever think that the Vice President of the United States, a person one heart beat away from leading this nation could be so arrogant and cruel of heart as to attack another American citizen in such a way, let alone one who has been a United States Senator for more than two decades and who has obviously more than satisfied the voters in his home state. Are these the values that we want in the (men or women) who are to lead this nation?

Mr. Bush's decision to invade Iraq may cost American taxpayers over one hundred and fifty to perhaps two hundred billion dollars before all is said and done. It is hard to relate to billions of dollars, when most Americans don't even have millions of dollars. When politicians in Washington throw these numbers around, as they often do, over time we become desensitized to what those numbers actually mean. We can think of the sum of one billion dollars being represented by one thousand suitcases, each filled with one million dollars. I was going to try to do a calculation for you here on my trusty calculator but my calculator will not accept a number higher than something a little over nine hundred and ninety-nine million dollars. It will be necessary to get to my computer to make this calculation. Two hundred billion dollars would purchase a new $10,000 economy car for twenty million American households. If a new hospital costs ten million dollars to build, two hundred billion dollars would create new hospitals in 20,000 communities across the United States. When Mr. Bush decided to invade Iraq, did he consider what it would cost each one of us? If he didn't, how can we trust him with the stewardship of our entire nation. If he did consider the costs to us of his decision, what in God's name does he think he is doing with our money?

How honest is the term compassionate conservatism when the Agriculture Department announced towards the end of last year that nearly twelve million American families were concerned about whether they had enough money to buy food, let alone other essentials.[28] Perhaps capital gains tax relief for some of us is simply more important than assuring the basic needs of the poorest of us. The Census Bureau reported in the year 2003 that there was a second annual increase in the number of Americans living in poverty and over two years that group had grown by three million more Americans living in poverty; while George Bush pushes for repeal of the Federal Estate Tax for the six percent of the wealthiest Americans in this country and income tax cuts for the middle class, which he makes available only by going out and borrowing the money in order make them. I have never used the hallucinogenic drug LSD, but doesn't this sound like a weird LSD trip? Our President borrows money, put us (our government) further in debt, and then claims that he has done us a favor!

In the movie, "The American President" Michael Douglas, playing the character of the President, refuses to join in the debate over his character. At the end of the movie, he eventually admits that being President, being the leader of the most powerful country in the free world, "is all about character." What does it tell us about the character of Mr. Bush and his Administration, that in order to silence a critic, someone within the Administration released the identity of his wife, who was an undercover CIA agent, her name, Valerie Plame.[29] Up until that time, her husband had been a rank-

and-file Republican, who simply decided to exercise his right as an American citizen to criticize the Bush Administration. What occurred seems to be in keeping with the initial objective of the Bush Administration, which was to label all criticism of their proposals, or actions, which they proposed to take after 9/11, as being unpatriotic. No President, in the history of this country, has ever so intentionally abused the concept of patriotism in an attempt to silence his critics. Without critical analysis and critical comment, freedom of expression in this country is worthless.

In terms of the management of the war in Iraq, disregarding for the moment whether the war was justified, it is important for all of us to understand the decisions being made by our President. If he is unwilling to listen to anyone else, this jeopardizes not only our troops in Iraq but also our position in the world. Listen to what Thomas Friedman of the *New York Times* had to say in an article carried by the *St. Petersburg Times* on October 24, 2003: "What in God's name are you doing forcing Iraqis to accept Turkish peace-keeping troops? Are you nuts? Not only will Turkish troops in Iraq alienate the Kurds, our best friends, but they will rile the Shiites and Sunnis as well. Honor is unusually important in

Iraqi society, and bringing in Turkish soldiers— Iraq's former colonizers - to order around Iraqis would be a disaster."[30]

The Pension Benefit Guarantee Corporation was established by Congress as the agency responsible for insuring retirement plans for forty-four million American workers and retirees. Last year, the head of that government agency stated that the collapse of the guarantee program is likely without re-structuring.[31] The Bush Administration's response to this crisis was to change the rules regarding pensions allowing companies to further under fund their pension programs, which will worsen the Pension Benefit Guarantee Corporation's solvency. Now that more companies will be permitted to under fund their pension plans, this will ultimately undermine the Pension Benefit Guarantee Corporation and could, in the future, require a taxpayer bailout.[32] Are these the types of decisions we want our President and his congressional leaders to make for us?

In a report originating from the *New York Times* and carried by my local newspaper, the *St. Petersburg Times*, in November of 2003, the Attorneys' General of New York, New Jersey and Connecticut came to the opinion that they had no choice but to initiate a new round of litigation "to force power plants to make billions of dollars of pollution control improvements after a decision by the Bush Administration to abandon more than fifty investigations into violations of the Clean Air Act."[33] According to a previous article originating from the *New York Times* and carried by *St. Petersburg Times* three days earlier, this statement was made: "Representatives of the utility industry had been among President Bush's campaign donors and a change in enforcement had been a top priority of their lobbyists."[34] In a column originating from the *Knight Ridder Newspapers* and carried in the *St. Petersburg Times*, this statement is made, "Civil enforcement of pollution laws peaked when the President's father George Bush, was in office from 1989 through 1993 and has fallen ever since, but it has plummeted since George W. Bush took office three years ago. That's according to records of seventeen different categories of enforcement activity obtained by *Knight Ridder* through the Freedom of Information Act."[35] In an *Associated Press* report carried by the *St. Petersburg Times*, it was stated in December of last year that: "The Bush administration is proposing to abandon the idea of treating mercury as a toxic substance requiring maximum pollution controls, favoring a plan instead that allows power plants to curtail emissions through a trading system."[36] This *Associated Press* report also indicates that a primary component of this rule change would also allow utilities to choose to purchase emissions credits instead of installing new equipment which would reduce mercury pollution. Doesn't this sound like something you would see at a carnival? It is the old shell game. You walk up to a gentleman who has a little ball to put under a shell, then you have to figure out which shell he is has moved it under. You start with one ball and three shells, and you wind up with one ball and three shells. Your position never improves. Why is Mr. Bush favoring the lobbying requests of the utility industry over the health, safety and welfare of every man, woman and child in the United States?

From a wire article submitted by the *Scripps Howard News Service*, March 20, 2004, "Forty-three states have issued fish-consumption advisories covering 500,000 miles of river and 12 million lakes. The advisories warn residents to avoid or restrict consumption of certain types of fish or fish from specific bodies of water because of mercury contamination."[37]   Pollution is also killing our oceans. Fertilizer and chemical run-offs have created dead zones where nothing will live. Oceanographer Sylvia Earle, speaking to the issue of pollution, toxic waste, and over fishing has said, "As compared to the 1950's, 90 percent of the grouper and snapper and other large fish are gone."[38]

If for any reason you just aren't willing to believe those news accounts, then perhaps you will believe some of the people who work for and support environmental protection organizations throughout the United States. In a recent Friends of the Earth letter "requesting additional membership funding," Brent Blackwelder, its President, stated "President Bush continues to be the worst President for the environment we've ever had." From the February 2004 newsletter to members of the organization known as the Union of Concerned Scientists, the President of the Union of Concerned Scientists states, "Despite claims that his Administration would make decisions about climate change that were science-based, the Bush Administration has suppressed the strong scientific consensus on this issue. For example, in June 2003, the White House tampered with the integrity of scientific analysis in the Environmental Protection Agency's annual report on the state of the environment. The White House demanded so many unsupported changes and qualified statements to the climate change section that EPA research scientists felt that it was no longer scientifically credible and deleted the entire section from the report." What Mr. Knobloch, President of this organization is talking about is Mr. Bush's request that any terms or references to global warming be eliminated or be replaced with substitute non-descriptive terms. In the same newsletter, Mr. Knobloch also states the following: "In the summer of 2002, the administration tampered with the integrity of a scientific advisory panel nominating process. An advisory panel to the Centers for Disease Control was expected to strengthen the federal standards to prevent "lead poisoning" because recent data showed the current standard was inadequate to protect young children from brain damage. Just before the panel was to convene, the administration took the extraordinary step of rejecting qualified researchers nominated by the agency's scientific staff—and appointing its nominees—two of whom it was later discovered had been hand-picked by the lead industry."

THE LEAGUE OF CONSERVATION VOTERS is an umbrella organization representing many state government and private environmental protection organizations. In a letter to members requesting additional funding, this organization had this to say: We are "...the organization that is using smart and strategic politics to fight the Bush Administration's attempt to dismantle our environmental laws. At stake is your health and the health of millions of Americans— the air you breath, the water you drink, America's forest, wildlife and wilderness areas. We have already launched a massive grass roots campaign to educate the public about President Bush's horrible environmental record." Still later in that letter, "The Bush Administration is clearly on the side of polluting special interest contributors and has allowed them to roll back America's environmental policies to benefit their bottom lines at the expense of our health and the environment."

In a letter from Robert F. Kennedy, Jr., Senior Attorney with the National Resources Defense Council: [this letter came out approximately three months prior to this coming November's 2004 National Elections] "The next ninety days will be 'do or die' for America's environment. Why? Because the White House and its executive agencies are now racing to put radical new policies in place that will let their corporate cronies poison our air, foul our water and devastate our wildlife for decades to come. This sweeping onslaught will cripple many of the safeguards that protect us from the very worst excesses of the oil, coal, logging, mining and chemical industries. It took thirty years to put these vital protections in place, but by the end of this year, this administration will be close to wiping them out. That is not exaggeration. That is not hyperbole. It is a fact."

This from a recent newsletter, requesting funding from William H. Meadows, President of the Wilderness Society: "The oil and gas companies have sympathetic friends in the White House and Congress. After all, Secretary of the Interior, Gail Norton, is a former lobbyist for a chemical company, and J. Steven Griles, the Deputy Secretary of the Interior, is a former lobbyist for the oil, gas and coal industries. Vice President Cheney, a former CEO of an oil-field service company, secretly met with Enron and other and gas companies while developing the administration's energy plan. So it is no surprise that the energy plan "pays back" big oil and the energy interests that lavished contributions on President Bush's Presidential campaign, with more tax breaks." As I mentioned earlier, attorneys, accountants and other professionals whose sworn duty it is to act in the best interest of those whom they represent are licensed to work in accordance with professional codes of conduct requiring that they avoid even the appearance of impropriety. When a President actually appoints as the head of a particular government department and the second in command of that same department, former lobbyists, who had so staunchly worked for the industries which they are now supposed to be regulating, hasn't the fox been let into the hen house? Is this responsible leadership? Is it responsible or honest leadership when these conflicts of interest are entirely ignored? How can we in good conscience re-elect anyone who uses slogans and catch phrases on a daily basis to direct our attention away from what he is really doing to us?

Just as Mr. Bush has ignored the immediate threat of a nuclear North Korea, a true rogue nation state, he has ignored what needs to be done, in cooperation with other nations in the world to protect the environment, the habitat of the human race. What Mr. Bush claims is not a problem, he has termed it "climate change" rather than global warming, is contradicted by scientists around the world."[39] By 2050, the scientists say, if current warming trends continue, 15 to 37 percent of the 1,103 species then studied may be doomed."[40] What happens to human beings when the plants and animals around them die off? Since Mr. Bush hasn't "attacked" this problem, he would rather that we not hear about it.

As Americans we take pride in the claim that ours is one of the best forms of government in the world. We expect, or perhaps demand, that our representatives in Congress and in the White House honestly pursue what is best for all of us and, treat us with respect, tell us everything that they know. It is the least that we expect in a free and democratic society. It is of great concern then when the White House, and specifically Vice President Cheney, refuses the requests of two groups that are on each end of the political spectrum, the Judicial Watch, a group considered to be on the right, and the Sierra Club, considered to be on the left of that spectrum. It was their simple request to know the identities of those with whom he met in the first few months of the Administration to form United States Energy Development Policy. This is something I think which is important for all of us to know. He refused their requests. This ultimately forced these organizations to file suit against him. Mr. Cheney did not accept the Federal District Court Judge's opinion that he must provide this information, and he appealed that decision. The appeals court agreed with the lower court and directed him to provide the information. Instead, he appealed again to the United States Supreme Court. Mr. Cheney, we as Americans want to know how our elected and appointed representatives are going about the process of making decisions which affect our future. If you had nothing to hide, there would be no reason to spend our tax dollars on legal fees to defend against the requests for information which have legitimately been put to you.

Let's also not forget about the disgraceful treatment of New York City residents by the Bush Administration after the twin towers were attacked and destroyed. The White House, through the Environmental Protection Agency, told New Yorkers that dust and debris was not a significant health concern for them. Excuse me? You could not even see through the stuff. Later that representation proved to be quite false.[41]

As Americans we value our Bill of Rights and all provisions within the United States Constitution, which serve to declare just what those rights are. However, we as Americans also take those rights for granted. We never expect our country to turn into a police state; we are of the feeling that it could never happen here, and certainly, it should never happen, at least not overnight. These are progressive matters, which have a tendency to creep up on us, and then when it is too late, it is too late. Nevertheless, they do in hindsight have an identifiable beginning.

Let me tell you a story. It's a good story. It is about Bob Jones, an American citizen traveling overseas. Upon his return home, he is picked up by authorities as a material witness in an alleged plot to acquire and detonate a small nuclear bomb within the United States. He is held, incommunicado, and this continues when he is moved to a prison located on a naval base. It's fortunate to only be a story. What is really unfortunate is that it is not a story. These are the facts in the case of <u>Rumsfeld v. Padilla</u>, 542 US _____ (2004) (see http://wid.ap.org - Supreme Court Decisions), except rather than Bob Jones, the victim of this assault upon all of our constitutional rights, is Jose Padilla.

This President and his administration has interred prisoners of war and called them enemy combatants, thereby denying them the rights under the Geneva Convention. They have also arrested resident aliens, immigrants, and even U.S. citizens and held them without the benefit of due process and without the benefit of counsel. Without the benefit of due process generally means that they can't walk into a United States court of any kind, deny their guilt, and then enlist the aid of others in defending themselves against the charges presented. Why not? Because many haven't been charged! If we allow Mr. Bush and his administration to get away with such actions, it becomes a significant political tool for any person who serves as President of the United States because he or she could then begin jailing all political opponents, claiming that they are enemy combatants or terrorists. This is especially horrific when those jailed are locked up without being able to contact family or friends. Even the United States Supreme Court, which stopped the vote count in the 2000 election and handed Mr. Bush his victory, could not refrain from holding this conduct of Mr. Bush to be impermissible.[42] The President cannot by executive decision remove the rights of a U.S. citizen or even a detainee, despite the government's reasoning that it must do so for reasons of national security.[43]

None of us desire to or could easily make a case for protecting the rights of a terrorist. However, once anyone is within American custody (whether an actual terrorist, suspected terrorist, enemy combatant, prisoner of war or held by any other designation), they should be entitled to an expectation that they will not be tortured. If we torture them, what becomes of our own citizens who are then captured by our enemies, and what happens to our decades old policy of claiming that we can morally tell another country, another dictator, another leader that he or she is violating the human rights of his or her citizens or detainees, if we do the same thing. It is for this reason that the Abu Ghraib prison scandal is so important and so incredibly injurious to our position throughout the world. The arrogance it took on the part of this administration to permit, or fail to prevent, such abuse and torture has to make you wonder what the current administration is truly capable of. In this country, we used to elect statesmen and men and women of integrity. What has become of us now?

I have a great deal of respect for two very different Presidents. One was Republican Dwight D. Eisenhower whose words are enshrined in the U.S. Holocaust Museum in Washington, D.C., where he has warned us against those who might come after him and deny that the holocaust ever occurred and who just as amazingly as President, tried to warn us about the power and influence of our own military/ industrial complex, a forewarning directed to the greed and avarice which can propel us into war, feed companies like Halliburton, and cause companies like Enron to collapse. The other one was someone who was ill-prepared for the Presidency, but who came from a part of our country pretty much known for its values. I speak of President Harry S. Truman from the State of Missouri. It was he who said that the buck stops here (with the president). If you look to George W. Bush, mistakes are always made by someone else. When it comes to intelligence, by his director of the CIA; when it comes to abuse of prisoners in Iraq, by his Secretary of Defense; when it comes to losing the moral high ground and the support of the world which we had after 9/11, it is not his fault, it is simply that they, the vast majority of world citizens, don't see things the way he does. Why should his view of the world be different than theirs? His father saw the importance of building a true coalition before invading Iraq in the first Gulf War. Yet, our current President Bush decided to basically go it alone when he invaded Iraq, and now he tells us that he should be rewarded with another term. Does that make any sense to you?

When we elected George Bush, we trusted that he was a good man and would do the right things for us. He was emboldened by universal American support after the 9/11 attacks, after easily breezing through Afghanistan. He then claimed that we had to attack Iraq. Of course, the reasons he gave for this pre-emptive strike have now proven to be false. After the commencement of the Iraqi War, Mr. Bush has done so many things wrong, that rather than decreasing the risk of terrorism to us, he has multiplied it a thousand fold. He has failed in over twenty-four months to locate and arrest or kill Osama Bin Laden, who is the acknowledged planner behind the 9/11 attacks, and this failure cannot be corrected by the selective timing of his arrest or capture, should George Bush, knowing where Osama Bin Laden is located, decide to pluck him out of a hat just in time for the November elections. His capture at this time would mean little or nothing. It is the successive and repetitive judgments of Mr. Bush and his administration, on domestic policy as well as foreign policy, which can leave no reasonable, prudent, introspective mind with any conclusion other than the fact that George W. Bush has done grave damage to our country.

If you have found nothing else in this chapter to be

disturbing, you should have been sitting in front of my television with me in either June or July of this year (2004). I was watching the news on CNN. This network was carrying a very brief report (or at least they were keeping it brief), but it was the most stunning and stupefying news report I have ever witnessed in my entire life. A bipartisan group (consisting of both Republicans and Democrats, who themselves were appointed by Republican Presidents and Democratic Presidents alike over the last 40 years) came together and formed a group calling themselves Diplomats and Military Commanders for Change (diplomatsforchange. com/press/press.html). They came together and signed a statement, basically addressed to the American people, asking that President George W. Bush not be re-elected. This group of 26 former Senior Diplomats and Military Commanders included Charles Freeman, former Ambassador to Saudi Arabia who had been appointed by George Bush's father when he was President; Stansfield Turner head of the CIA under President Carter; Admiral William Crowe, Chairman of the Joint Chiefs of Staff under former President Ronald Reagan; Marine Corp General Joseph Hoar, named by George Bush's father when he was President, to lead U.S. forces in the

Middle East; and General Merrill A. (Tony) McPeak, former Chief of Staff of the United States Air Force, former Oregon State Chairman of the Dole-Kemp campaign in 1996, and a member of Veterans for Bush in 2002. The signed letter was presented to news reporters at the National Press Club on June 16, 2004. Opening the conference was Ambassador Phyllis Oakley, who explained "To be involved in an act that will be seen by many as political if not partisan is for many of us a new experience. As career government officials, we have served loyally both Republican and Democratic administrations. . . For many of us, such an overt step is hard to do and we have made our decisions after deep reflection. We believe we have as good an understanding as any of our citizens, of basic American interest. Over nearly half a century we have worked energetically in all regions of the world, often in very difficult circumstances, to build, piece by piece, a structure of respect and influence for the United States that has served our country very well over the last sixty years. Today we see that structure crumbling under an administration blinded by ideology, and a callous indifference to the realities of the world around it. Never before have so many of us felt the need for a major change in the direction of our foreign policy. . . Everything we have heard from our friends abroad on every continent suggests to us the lack of confidence in the present administration in Washington is so profound that a whole new team is needed to repair the damages."[44]

At no time in our history as a country, have men and women from both parties had the courage and felt the need to join together to stop the utter destruction of the relationships, which our country has fostered with other members of the world over the last sixty years. If up until now, you have believed spokespersons for the Bush Administration, their political spin-masters, and what cannot be called anything other than actual propaganda, you must understand how hard it was for these former Ambassadors and Military Commanders to share with us the benefits of their experience and the discouragement which each of them feels. We cannot allow George Bush and his administration to destroy everything which we have accomplished throughout the world since World War II. It would be morally and socially unconscionable for us to allow them to do anymore damage.

I started off this chapter discussing Catholic Social

Conscience, which we all know as Christian Social Conscience. Even though the majority of the challenges within this book are directed to persons of the Catholic faith, I find myself not thinking of myself as a Catholic American, but as an American. My grandparents, on either side of the family, came to this country nearly a century ago looking for the American dream. They produced children, who produced children (which include my generation) who so much wanted to be a part of this country. Very few of the customs and none of the language was passed down to us, because we were to be Americans. I ask you now, not as Catholics, not as Christians, not as members of any other faith, but as Americans to do now and forever, what is best, what is right, and what a well-formed social conscience requires. Vote not as a Democrat or as a Republican, but as an American of conscience, who votes for the benefit of our community as a whole.

CHAPTER IX

HOW TO RESPOND TO LIES ABOUT US

Beware of the "Claim-to-be-Christians" who are outside of Christ's Church. They may be of the type who go door to door and claim to be the true Disciples of Christ, or they may be of the "saved" variety that grinds all of the "non-saved" beneath their heels. The latter is a "Born-again," better than any Catholic, and better than any of the members of main line Christian denominations. He believes that because he has accepted Jesus Christ as his personal Savior, he is thereby saved and that all of the rest of us are the pitiable unclean. Here is one of their stories: This Born Again is a doctor, an extremely successful one, which he attributes to being saved. As a saved Christian, he expects to be blessed with worldly treasures and believes that such is Christ's approval of him and of his conduct. He employs numerous physicians at his medical center, and when he determines which ones are Catholic, he directs his finance department to delay their salary checks. He continues this for several months in the hope that they will leave his practice and eventually they do.

If sued, they know that he will claim that they were lazy or incompetent. Rather than have their reputations smeared, they leave and never receive their rightful compensation. He feels justified now, for they have left, it hasn't cost him anything, and he believes that Christ has once again anointed him in battle, as he has devastated another nemesis of Christ, the Catholic.

The Born Again has made a judgment. Yet without knowing the mind of God, and none of us do, he refuses to acknowledge that his judgment may be flawed, as he is flawed. If he ever looks at the teachings of Matthew Chapter 7, 1-5; he does not see himself, as that chapter is pretty clear: "Stop judging, that you may not be judged. For as you judge, so will you be judged, and the measure with which you measure will be measured out to you. Why do you notice the splinter in your brother's eye, but do not perceive the wooden beam in your own eye? How can you say to your brother, 'Let me remove that splinter from your eye while the wooden beam is in your eye?' You hypocrite, remove the wooden beam from your eye first; then you will see clearly to remove the splinter from your brother's eye." [He can't see that the Word is speaking of him.] "Not everyone who says to me,

'Lord, Lord,' will enter the kingdom of heaven, but only the one who does the will of my Father in heaven. Many will say to me on that day, 'Lord, Lord, did we not prophesy in your name? Did we not drive out demons in your name? Did we not do mighty deeds in your name? Then I will declare to them solemnly, 'I never knew you. Depart from me you evildoers." Mt 7, 21-23.   He will never understand that he is the modern day Pharisee who thinks that he can judge others as well or better than God. He takes this judgment upon himself never realizing that the gospel of Matthew was meant for him. "For as you judge, so will you be judged, and the measure with which you measure will be measured out to you." Mt 7, 2.

When the "Claim-to-be-Christian" satanizes Christ's Church on earth, he blasphemes the Holy Spirit and, thereby, has sealed his own fate. "Amen, I say to you, all sins and all blasphemies that people utter will be forgiven them. But who ever blasphemes against the holy Spirit will never have forgiveness, but is guilty of an everlasting sin." Mark 3, 28-29. When the modern day Pharisee lays down his own law and states that "unless as an adult you accept Jesus Christ as your personal Savior" you cannot be saved, he presumes to be greater than God. A parent is authorized to declare the infant brought before the baptismal font, as a child of God. It is the magnificence of God through whom the parent can save his child. Is it then the position of the "Born-Again Christian" that God cannot so love?

As Catholics, we believe that our salvation is through Jesus Christ and that baptism seals us with his love. We also believe that once "saved" in this way, we can discard this gift by how we conduct ourselves through our lives. In that regard, never were more profound the words "actions speak louder than words." As Catholics, conducting ourselves as Christ would prefer that we do, is no small matter. When someone says that it isn't easy being Catholic, they usually mean that the "Good News" brings with it responsibility and sacrifice, which at times may seem terribly outside of our reach to achieve or impossible to endure. Then our hearts remind us that although we are finite and limited in capacity, the Lord is with us and for Him nothing is impossible.

What else do those who blaspheme the Holy Spirit say about his Church and his people, "Oh Catholics are not true Christians, they are idol worshipers." You can lie all that you want, you can distort the truth, and you can mislead the unchurched, who look to you because you claim to be a Christian Minister; but God who sees all understands your deceit and will punish you accordingly. We Catholics adorn our houses of worship, our Churches, with statues of people who have gone before us. These often represent Mary, the Mother of God, or Joseph, Christ's early stand-in human father. Others represent one or more of the Apostles or other devout Christians whom we believe may have lived extraordinary lives and may be considered saints. We do not worship the figurines. Like the photograph of a loved one who has died before us, and which we keep to remind us of that person, the statue reminds us of them as well. As you can observe from the creed of our faith, the Nicene Creed, we believe in the communion of saints, that those who have gone before us are not just laying on clouds or flopping around on angel-like wings, but that they, being closer to God, can also pray in communion with us to God. So, stop trying to tear down Christ's Church on earth with your lies, for God neither deceives nor is deceived. He has called over one billion Catholic people to Him throughout the world and the truth of His message lives on.

We too must guard against undue pride. We belong to

the Church which Christ himself established and, yes, we believe Catholicism to be the one true faith, but despite the fact that Jesus said "that all who come to the Father must come through me," how do we know what He meant by "me." The Holy Trinity, Father, Son and Holy Spirit, are beyond complete understanding. Perhaps through "me" includes through other religious figures in history who have taught similarly, and who drew people to the same fundamental belief that God loves His creation and wants them to be with Him throughout eternity. The Jews are referred to in Scripture as God's chosen people; once a chosen people, why not always a chosen people? Likewise, we can neither condemn nor reject those who follow Mohammad or Buddha. We must separate these people of faith from any clerics, who bastardize the true meaning of religion. When acting honestly, the message is the same; love one another. Only when religion is perverted or subverted to the objective of gaining power on earth, should its legitimacy be challenged and it message controverted.

CHAPTER X:

ANSWERS TO PRESSING ISSUES

A. MARRIED PRIESTS

This is certainly not very scientific, but I can't remember ever speaking to a member of the laity within the Catholic Church who disagreed with the proposition that priests should be allowed to marry. According to the February 1999 issue of *U.S. Catholic Magazine*, eighty percent of its readers who responded to a survey agreed that mandatory celibacy for Catholic priests should be abolished. What many of you may not be aware of is the double standard which presently exists. The Catholic Church actively encourages married Protestant ministers to come back to the Church and be ordained as Catholic priests. After ordainment, their marital status remains unchanged.

According to John Horan, also writing in the same issue of the *U.S. Catholic Magazine*, "For the first twelve centuries of church practice, thirty-nine popes were married in addition to many priests and bishops. Three popes (Anastasius I, St. Hormidas, and Sergius III) produced pope sons of their own, two of whom went on to be declared saints (St. Innocent I and St. Silverius)." Mr. Horan also indicates in his article that it was Pope Gregory VI in the eleventh century who required pledges of celibacy prior to ordination and that this pope was accredited with stating as a reason "the Church cannot escape from the clutches of the laity unless priests first escape the clutches of their wives."[45] Last summer, the summer of 2003, a large group of priests, numbering in excess of 160, were much maligned for coming together, signing and submitting letters to the President of U.S. Conference of Catholic Bishops, which is Bishop Wilton Gregory, stating "we urge that from now on celibacy be optional, not mandatory, for candidates for the Diocesan Roman Catholic Priesthood.[46]

In an article which he wrote for the June 30, 2003 edition of *Newsweek*, Tom Hogan, who describes himself as a Roman Catholic Seminary dropout, in referring to the Church's response to the pedophilia scandals, states, "This is, after all, Catholicism's Enron, where insiders knew all along what was going on and wondered when the rest of the world would notice—or care." Mr. Hogan's impression of his 1970's experience in the seminary is that there were far too many seminarians who did not hold the true calling of their profession; that too many of them are still in positions of authority within the Church and are the ones resisting change; and that homosexuality within the priesthood was an "open secret." All good reasons for inviting back former priests, who only left the priesthood to be married. This could be not only a short-term, but perhaps a longer term solution to the vocations problem, while the Church then dedicates its efforts to reviewing all recruiting, admissions, and training practices within its seminaries.

[In case you've missed them, the following materials, which appeared in Chapter V, are reprinted here for your convenience.]

This is a lonely world; a cruel world; a vicious world; one which it is impossible or nearly impossible to travel alone. Very few are capable of living a celibate life. It must no longer be mandatory. For those few who can attain it in all of its purity, they should be commended. But even for them, it should be aspirational. The celibacy debate has raged for centuries. It is time to stop debating it. It is nearly impossible to overcome the strongest of all human emotions, the human sex drive. We have been pre-designed and pre-engineered as sexual beings; not something that we can merely wish away. Priests who would be better priests if married should be allowed to marry, rather than be forced out of the priesthood. Those who have been forced out because of marriage should be welcomed back. There is no valid reason for these men to be punished any longer. Our God is not a jealous God. He would welcome happier, healthier, family-oriented priests. He is willing to share Himself with them and their families.

On the other hand, if you can maintain your vow of celibacy, commit yourself solely to Christ, and to his Church, then you should do so. If you are convinced that your calling can be bettered by a solitary commitment to God and the Body of Christ, undiluted by the responsibilities inherent in a relationship with a spouse or children, then all of the power of God and our prayers and support shall be with you. May God bless you and keep you with Him all of the days of your life. But don't claim that yours is the only way. Welcome those who wish to partner with both God and another human being.

B. HOW SHOULD WE TREAT OUR GAY AND LESBIAN BRETHREN

There is a simple answer to that question, not one which the Church hierarchy I imagine will find to be all that simple. Since we are the Church established by Jesus Christ, we should be welcoming our gay and lesbian brethren with open arms. Even if the heterosexual Body of Christ is uncomfortable in experiencing physical signs of affection between members of the same sex. It would, of course, be easier if gays and lesbians would act in our presence as if they were sexually neutral, but I imagine that would be asking for more than we are entitled to. Perhaps if we simply restricted marriage to its traditional sense, a relationship between a man and a woman, and reconsidered the importance to gay and lesbians of having their civil unions recognized, we could take a long first step in this area. Before that happens, the Church is going to have to make a decision which it seems at this time it is unprepared to do based upon recent statements issued by the Vatican. And that is whether homosexuality is a "nature," the same as heterosexuality. If the Church decides, along the lines of what I believe the scientific community has already established, that homosexuality is genetic, not something you choose for yourself, then I don't think the Church any longer can draw a distinction between homosexuals and heterosexuals. Of course, the next logical step would be if you cannot draw distinctions between homosexuality and heterosexuality because of genetic predisposition, then how can you within the Church deny some of your members the right to be married within the Church. This is probably from where the sticking point comes. Frankly, it is not an easy issue. Of those of us who are in a heterosexual marriage, we really can't conceive of anything else and, to us, it is the only thing that seems natural and to be called a marriage.

Where does the Church go from there? Can it ever offer a sacramental union between two men or between two women, without actually and eventually calling it a marriage? Our literal "Claim-to-be-Christians" will never be able to accept homosexuals within their congregation because they believe that homosexuality and sodomy are specifically prohibited in the statements made within the Scriptures. What they don't seem to realize, is that God may very well have been speaking about persons having sex by choice with another adult or child of the same sex, and that perhaps this was the primary focus of those directives. Considering the likelihood that many men have entered the priesthood in the Catholic Church over the centuries with the hope that their vow of celibacy would permit them to, in some way, repress their own homosexual nature, it is difficult to understand then why the Church is not taking a more conciliatory position with respect to this type of sexual relationship. This is an area for which we will have to continue to pray and work harder at finding a solution; a coming to terms with our own predispositions and what we consider to be a marriage. Unfortunately, the Vatican's most recent statement, "Considerations Regarding Proposals To Give Recognition To Unions Between Homosexual Persons," approved by Pope John Paul II and signed by Cardinal Joseph Ratzinger and Archbishop Angelo Amato, concludes that "for homosexuals, abstinence is the only solution, and that marriage exists solely between a man and a woman." Certainly, heterosexuals can accept this teaching, but it doesn't do much to help our gay and lesbian brethren. Here is the entire conclusion of that document: "The church teaches that respect for homosexual persons cannot lead in any way to approval of homosexual behavior or to legal recognition of homosexual unions. The common good requires laws recognize, promote, and protect marriage as the basis of the family, the primary unit of society. Legal recognition of homosexual unions, placing them on the same level as marriage, would mean not only the approval of deviant behavior but the consequence of making it a model in present day society, but would also obscure basic values that belong to the common inheritance of humanity. The church cannot fail to defend these values for the good of men and women and for the good of society itself." The first part of this conclusion makes sense (respect for homosexual persons), but the second part is a little difficult to understand. How would legalizing homosexual unions obscure basic values that belong to the common inheritance of humanity? Although, I am not a proponent of gay and lesbian marriages, for the same reason most of us are not in favor of gay and lesbian marriages (we are not gay or lesbian), I don't believe that this document issued by the Vatican does much to foster the type of understanding and love that we are to have for each of our brethren, all given existence by the same Creator.

The issues concerning the rights of homosexuals are perhaps key to understanding that there always needs to be separation between church and state. Here, the Church is not willing to recognize the rights of those who have a different sexual orientation than that which is described in Scriptures as necessary for procreation. On the other hand the United States Supreme Court ruling in the case of <u>Lawrence v. Texas</u> 539 U.S. ____ (2003), declared the sodomy statute in Texas to be unconstitutional and that homosexual acts done in private are constitutionally protected.   Without separation of church from state, you could never have such a result. The extraordinarily conservative and narrow-minded would have no problem through their churches denying rights of equal protection under the United States Constitution to homosexuals, or the right of privacy or any other rights under the constitution. The only problem with that thinking is that this country, the United States of America, was established upon the proposition that the founders did not want to carry over with them to this continent the interference and influence of any church upon the governance of the state. For over two hundred years, this separation has worked pre-eminently well. It is only in recent times, that certain religious elements, not just within the Catholic Church, but also within a number of Protestant denominations, have discovered that this could be an avenue by which to exert political influence. It is from those same elements, if they had their own way, that they would reinstitute Prohibition from the early part of the last century, if they could, prohibiting even those of us who have an occasional beer or glass of wine from drinking at all, and whatever other religious or "moral" requirements, which they are excited about at the time. To all of them it must be stated clearly, that for freedom of religion to continue to exist in this country and elsewhere in the world, each church, each religion, each denomination, must stay out of politics and must not fall into the trap of saying that if you belong to this particular religion, you have to act in political life or vote in political life in a certain way, because that is simply a narrow analysis of the emotional and psychological feelings that go into making decisions about significant issues, which emotions and feelings must be respected by those who hold contrary opinions. If churches in general, are ever to respect the dignity of a human being, then they must respect each person's freedom to choose between what is essentially good and what is essentially evil, while at the same time providing moral certitude "in those situations where it is humanly possible to do so" that one behavior or another is preferred. With the way in which the Catholic Church in recent history has operated its own affairs, we certainly do not want it now telling us in our civil lives how to operate ours.

C. CULTS

A cult is generally understood as an organization of some sort, whether small or large, which maintains so much control over its members that they are not free to think for themselves. Sometimes cult membership continues for decades before the person actually realizes what has been going on and leaves that cult in order to testify to the world about how easy it was to be controlled. Certain cults have become so large within this country and around the world that only an organization as large as the Church might have an opportunity to stop them. My preference is to deal with cults generally, and to not name names, because some of them have become so powerful, so veracious, and so vicious that once they identify their detractors, they apply all of the formidable resources available to them, including, but not limited to, stalking that person and invading his or her privacy to the greatest extent they can possibly manage. If these cultists are being kept from an understanding of who Jesus Christ really is, why He came into this world, and why His life was sacrificed, then the established Church or perhaps all of the established churches should have some concern for the souls of these people. Some concern should mean formulating responses, establishing task forces, training deprogramming units, providing financial assistance and helping in any other way necessary to reclaim these souls whom God has created. To leave certain cults unchecked, is an invitation to the cults to plunder from among those who do not exhibit characteristics of self-confidence, strength, moral or psychological certitude of conduct, or a general understanding of where they fit in and where their place is in this world. Normally, when you wait for something to grow large enough that it becomes a visible blip on your radar, you then have some real problems defending against it.

D. HOW THE CHURCH MUST LEAD THE FIGHT AGAINST SECULARISM

Unfortunately, the Church agrees that it should lead the fight against secularism, but interprets its response to secularism to mean telling men and women who seek political office that they are not good Catholics unless they act or vote in a certain way in legislative chambers. The leaders of the Church then state that failure to comply will result in your being denied Communion. What's next on the horizon; are you going to ex-communicate too? If that is the case, you should most likely ask the vast majority of Catholics to leave the Catholic Church, because the Body of Christ does not desire for the Church to interfere with the matters of state. Teach us, encourage us, instruct us on what you believe is morally correct, but don't threaten us if we don't do what you direct. Threats come from desperate men. If you are that desperate, then you have already lost the battle. No, the true fight against secularism is to begin again the war that the Church has already lost, which was the war against selfishness, commercialism, pornography, exploitation of men and women around the world who are basically powerless and disenfranchised (not limited to immigrant workers and sweatshop workers), over-consumption, gluttony, lack of honesty, lack of integrity, lack of reconciliation, and the failure to consider misrepresentations and omissions any longer to be lies. Perhaps it is difficult for the Church to begin a new war against secularism because the Church has become so secular. If it has, then none of us are without fault. If the Church has become more secular, it is because we have all become more secular. We must all begin again, starting first with the Church cleaning its own house, getting its affairs in order, sharing decision making with the laity, and involving the laity in its future.

E. ABORTION

[With the exception of the last paragraph which is new, this material is reprinted here from Chapter I for the convenience of the reader.]

Then, as if to add insult to injury, and further undermine the laity's faith in your leadership, you Bishops within the United States issued a statement on Friday, June 16, 2004 entitled "Catholics in Political Life,"[47] likely to be looked upon as the single most significant mistake ever made by United

States Catholic Bishops, only to be exceeded by the covering up of child abuse within the Church and the reassignment of sexual deviants to other parishes without notice given to those parishes. The present perception is that this body within the Church has lost its way, but because of their current positions, must immediately rescind this statement.

When the Pharisees attempted to trap Jesus, they asked him, "Is it lawful to pay the census tax to Caesar or not?" Jesus said to them, "Show me the coin that pays the census tax." Then they handed him the Roman coin. He said to them, "Whose image is this and whose inscription? They replied, Caesar's." At that he said to them, "Then repay to Caesar what belongs to Caesar and to God what belongs to God." Mt 22, 17-22. Jesus never interfered with the civil authority of His time. Although the Jews were looking for a military messiah who would overthrow the civil government of the Romans, which they felt was oppressive, He never said, "Use my teachings to control political figures." The United States was founded by people whose heartfelt belief was that there should be no state sponsored or approved religion, for without this prohibition, one church or another would grow in such power that it would dictate to the civil leaders what should be done, and then that country would have a defacto state religion. It is one thing to state that a Catholic's view of abortion, if contrary to the Church, should be re-examined. It is quite another to attempt to intrude into politics and civil governance by threatening political candidates with refusal of Holy Communion. Elsewhere in this book, I label the born-again Christian as the modern day Pharisee. It saddens me to the depths of my soul that our Bishops desire to compete for this title. As Church leaders, it is your responsibility to show by your actions humility, understanding, and forgiveness. You show no understanding of what a woman goes through when she is faced with this decision. If abortion is such a terrible thing, and certainly it can be, then why haven't you reached out more visibly and with more resources to those facing this decision, so that counseling and financial support could be provided to convince more women not to make this choice. Why instead do you seek to judge when Christ Himself has told you not to?

Does not Matthew say in Chapter 7, Verses 1 through 5 "Stop judging, that you may not be judged. For as you judge, so will you be judged, and the measure with which you measure will be measured out to you. Why do you notice the splinter in your brother's eye, but do not perceive the wooden beam in your own eye? How can you say to your brother, 'Let me remove that splinter from your eye, while the wooden beam is in your own eye? You hypocrite, remove the wooden beam from your eye first; then you will see clearly to remove the splinter from your brother's eye." How can you possibly deny Holy Communion to political candidates who support a woman's right to make this decision? When you judge them unworthy to receive Holy Communion (your statement says that Bishops and Priests can deny Holy Communion to these people) you are judging what is in a person's heart. How can you know what is in a person's heart? Such a judgment is reserved to Jesus Christ Himself and not to you. How can any priest see into anyone's heart? How could any member of the clergy presume to know only what Jesus knows? This is where the folly of your statement lies. You are so focused on the evil of abortion that you have allowed Satan himself to draw you into the trap of fanaticism.

Since when are crises of conscience to be resolved by legislation rather than by the penitent sinner alone in communication with his or her Savior? Abortion is an extremely important issue, not just to the Church, but to society in general; it is not one to be decided solely by a group of men who themselves have never been faced by the decision. There are times when as a result of rape, incest, or threat of death to the mother, it cannot be said with any moral certitude that abortion is clearly against the will of God. If freedom of choice is as essential to Christian theology as it is, for only with freedom of choice can one understand the difference between good and evil, then when there is no choice, when the will is overcome by someone else, as in rape or incest, it cannot be said that abortion is then morally objectionable. How do we know this? Because none of us are perfect, not you, not me, not the clergy, and not our legislators. Because we are imperfect and cannot know the mind of God, we have no right to use religion to threaten politicians or to interfere with political discussions which must take place on this most important issue.

As much as Catholics may wish to see the elimination of abortions, we must consider that we are dealing with two lives here, that of the mother as well as of the child which she is carrying. We cannot on the basis of religion, simply ignore her rights and elevate those of her unborn child beyond hers. That is why this issue is so difficult, both to discuss and to resolve. As much as we would like to protect the life of the unborn child, how can we in good conscience use religion to legislate away a medical procedure which may be necessary to save the mother's life. This is an issue, as there are other issues in our lives, which cannot be adequately addressed by constitutional prohibitions or by legislation. They must be left to be resolved between the woman electing an abortion and her God, for we as Catholics know that it is not beyond the measure of Christ's love to forgive this woman the decision which she feels that she must make. This is a time for us to recognize our human frailty and fallibility; to recognize the fact that whether you are pro-life or pro-choice you may both ultimately be wrong, especially in the way that you treat each other.

What makes the abortion issue even more confusing is that, "The Church has never definitively stated when the ensoulment of the human embryo takes place. It remains an open question."[48] This from Father Tadeusz Pacholczyk, one of the Church's experts on this issue. Apparently when the human embryo receives its soul has not been decided, even though most Catholics have previously presumed that it takes place at the moment of fertilization.

CHAPTER XI:
THE LORD OF THE DANCE (MUSIC FOR ALL SEASONS)

If you have experienced Michael Flatley's theater production, *Lord of the Dance*, then you know how exciting certain combinations of music and dance can be. When we worship the Father, the Son, and the Holy Spirit at Mass, we celebrate God's new covenant with His people in the consecration of Jesus' sacrifice, and how He asked us to remember this sacrifice through the Last Supper. For those like me who just can't sing, it may be difficult to relate to the importance of song as part of the worship service. I have struggled with this myself for many decades and unless someone pays close attention to me, I can now generally mimic the words pretty well. It is extremely uplifting to participate in the Mass in this way; to not only articulate the necessary responses, but also to sing praise to the Lord. I invite you to try it, as you may well find that you enjoy it.

The songs which I am about to list for you are favorites of mine and of my wife, and we find ourselves at home in those parishes we visit from time to time, across the country, which utilize at least two of these out of a total of four or five music selections for that particular Mass. I invite you to consider them for use in your church or as a guide in choosing recorded music which you may find satisfying.

1. "Gather Us In" by Marty Haugen

2. "City of God" by Dan Schutte

3. "Here I Am Lord" by Dan Schutte

4. "Taste And See" by James E. Moore, Jr.

5. "I Am The Bread Of Life" by Suzanne Tollan, RSM

6. "Gift Of Finest Wheat" by Robert E. Kreutz

7. "One Bread, One Body" by John Foley, S.J.

8. "They'll Know We Are Christians"
        by Peter Scholtes

9. "Come Holy Ghost" by Lombillotte

10. "The Spirit Is A Movin" by Carey Landry

11. "Be Not Afraid" by Bob Dufford, S.J.

12. "Though The Mountains May Fall"
        by Dan Schutte

13. "On Eagles Wings" by Michael Joncas

14. "You Are Near" by Dan Schutte

15. "For You Are My God" by John Foley, S.J.

16. "O God, Our Help In Ages Past" by St. Anne

17. "Blest Be The Lord" by Dan Schutte

18. "How Great Thou Art" by Stuart K. Hine

19. "Prayer Of St. Frances" by Sebastian Temple

20. "Let There Be Peace On Earth" by Sy Miller
    and Bill Jackson

21. "Peace Is Flowing Like A River" by Carey Landry

22. "Shepherd Me, O God" by Marty Haugen

23. "The Cry of the Poor" by John Foley, S.J.

24. "Whatsoever You Do" by Willard F. Jabusch

25. "Lord Of The Dance Shaker Song"
    by Sydney Carter

26. "We Are The Light Of the World"
    by Jean Anthony Greif

27. "Soon And Very Soon" by William F. Smith

28. "Glory And Praise To Our God" by Dan Schutte

29. "Sing To The Mountains" by Bob Dufford, S.J.

30. "Joyful, Joyful, We Adore Thee"
    by Henry Van Dyke

31. "All the Ends of the Earth" by Bob Dufford, S.J.

32. "Sing A New Song" by Dan Schutte

33. "Isaiah 49" by Carey Landry

34. "I Have Loved You" by Michael Joncas

35. "Rain Down" by Jaime Cortez

36. "Like A Shepherd" by Bob Dufford, S.J.

37. "Morning Has Broken" by Eleanor Farjeon

38. "This Day God Gives Me" by St. Patrick
     and James D. Quinn

39. "America, The Beautiful" by Katherine L. Bates
     and Samuel A. Ward

40. "America" by Samuel F. Smith

41. "Keep In Mind " by Lucien Deiss, CSSP

42. "Seek The Lord" by Roc O'Connor, S.J.

43. "Turn To Me" by John Foley, S.J.

44. "Remember Your Love" by Darryl Ducote
     and Gary Daigle

45. "Hosea" by Weston Priory

46. "Save Us, O'Lord" by Bob Dufford, S.J.

47. "Salve, Regina" by Contractus/Ford

48. "Ave Maria" by Paul Ford

49. "Hail Mary: Gentle Woman" by Carey Landry

50. "Sing of Mary" by Roland F. Palmer

51. "Hail Holy Queen Enthroned Above"
     by Hermann Contractus

52. "Immaculate Mary" by Irwin Dulutsch

53. "Hail Holy Queen" by Melchoir Herald

54. "The King Of Glory" by Willard F. Jabusch

55. "Alleluia! Sing To Jesus" by Dix/Prichard

56. "Praise To the Lord" by Joachim Neonder

57. "We Gather Together" by Theodore Baker

58. "Holy God, We Praise Thy Name" by Ignaz Franz

CHAPTER XII:
AN INVITATION TO UNITY

All Christians are members of the universal Church and hopefully will find it within themselves to reunite again in the not-to-distant future. For those of you of other faiths, please keep us in your prayers that we might get our own house in order so as to be able to invite you back into it. Certainly, our differences are not that extreme that we could not be united now if we all desired to be. We also understand and acknowledge that customs and routine are difficult to deviate from, especially when we have spent all of our lives doing things in a certain way. Nevertheless, let us pray together that unity will be found before too much more time goes by.

ENDNOTES

[1]Full text of the U.S. Bishop's Statement can be found in *Our Sunday Visitor* newspaper, July 4, 2004, p. 8.

[2]T. Bokenkotter, *A Concise History of the Catholic Church*, Doubleday, New York, 1990, at p. 40.

[3]Ibid., p. 151.

[4]*The Saint Joseph Edition of THE NEW AMERICAN BIBLE*, Catholic Book Publishing Co., New York, 1987.

[5]In T*he Catechism of the Catholic Church*, Liguori Publications, Liguori, Mo.,© 1994, United States Catholic Conference, there are no index references to Tithe, Tithing, Stewardship, or Sacrificial Giving.

[6] Editorial, "Sugarcoated Credibility," *St. Petersburg Times*, September 13, 2003, Section A, p. 12.

[7]This information can also be found in wire service article from K*night Ridder Newspapers* entitled, "Scientists raise criticisms of Bush's policies," printed in the *St. Petersburg Times*, February 19, 2004.

[8] *Cox News Service* report entitled, "Greenspan sees

peril in deficits," printed in the *St. Petersburg Times*, May 7, 2004, Section D, p. 1.

In a column written by Congressman Jim Davis entitled, "The federal debt does matter," *St. Petersburg Times*, March 17, 2004, Section A, p. 15, Greenspan is quoted as saying, "History suggests that an abandonment of fiscal discipline will eventually push up interest rates, crowd out capital spending, lower productivity growth, and force harder choices upon us in the future."

[9] Article from *Knight Ridder Newspapers* entitled, "Medicare saga gets messier," printed in the *St. Petersburg Times*, March 21, 2004, Section A, p. 6.

[10]Editorial, "Medicare's delayed reality," *St. Petersburg Times*, February 2, 2004, Section A, p. 8.

[11]Mr. Terrence A. Gourdine of Clearwater, Florida I think put it best when he sent a letter to the *St. Petersburg Times* which was published in a December 2003 edition entitled, "The Real Medicare Beneficiary." Mr. Gourdine writes: "People who continue to defend George W. Bush's Medicare overhaul and prescription drug program and who actually believe that this change primarily benefits average senior citizens should answer just three simple questions:

• Why did every major health insurance company, drug company and hospital chain enthusiastically support the Medicare overhaul and drug program?

• Why did these same insurance, drug and health care providers spend so many hundreds of millions of dollars to lobby Congress for its passage?

• Why do health insurance companies, drug companies and large hospital chains so generously give vast amounts of PAC money to the President, to Republicans in general, and to members of Congress who support this issue?

If your conclusion is that the "insurance, drug and hospital industries are basically altruistic, having only an interest in championing the welfare of America's senior citizens, and therefore simply helped to push a "good bill" through Congress, your path is clear." In November 2004, you should vote for George Bush and every Republican who continues to support the "good works" of these groups.

On the other hand, if you resolved that these are actually self-serving "special interest" groups who have the ability to "buy" Congress so they can reap huge "and often unearned" profits, and who will actually become the greatest beneficiaries of the President's and the Republicans' actions then, in November 2004, you should vote for every Democrat on the ballot." [Reprinted with the permission of Mr. Gourdine.]

[12] E. J. Dionne, Jr., Washington Post Writers Group, "Drug bill voting process," *St. Petersburg Times*, November 26, 2003, Section A, p. 14.

[13] Joseph Hoar and Richard Klass, "Iraq war has made America less safe," Special to the *Washington Post* printed in the *St. Petersburg Times*, October 14, 2003, Section A, p. 8.

Benjamin Schwartz, "Truth doesn't matter in matters of war," Special to the *Los Angeles Times* printed in the *St. Petersburg Times*, November 3, 2003, Section A.

Bill Maxwell, "After pigeon inspections, Bush eats crow," *St. Petersburg Times*, March 3, 2004, Section A, p. 15.

William Raspberry, "Doling out the benefit of the doubt," Washington Post Writers Group printed in the *St. Petersburg Times*, February 2, 2004, Section A, p. 9.

David S. Broder, "Our abstract discourse ignores Iraq war reality," Washington Post Writers Group printed in the *St. Petersburg Times*, March 21, 2004, Section P, p. 3.

[14] "Ex-arms hunter: U.S. spies failed," *New York Times* article printed in the *St. Petersburg Times*, January 26, 2004, Section A, p. 2.

Editorial, "Those missing weapons," *St. Petersburg Times*, January 27, 2004, Section A, p. 6.

[15] Jackson Diehl, "Who foresaw Iraq errors? Lots of folks," *Washington Post* article printed in the *St. Petersburg Times*, January 6, 2004, Section A, p. 6.

[16] George F. Will, "Don't count on Iraq oil revenues settling our tab," Washington Post Writers Group printed in the *St. Petersburg Times*, October 12, 2003, Section D,

p. 3.

[17] "Iraq," *St. Petersburg Times*, October 29, 2003, Section A.

[18] Robert D. Novak, "Bush's support wanes in Capitol angst," carried in *St. Petersburg Times*, March 4, 2004, Section A, p. 12.

[19] IRC § 2010.

[20] "Universal Health Care Coverage," in the *Almanac of Policy Issues*, taken from a US Census Bureau Press Release, September 30, 2002, found at this URL http://www.policyalmanac.org/health /universal_health.html.

[21] Jonathan Weisman, "U.S. Incomes Fell, Poverty Rose in 2002," *Washington Post*, September 27, 2003, Section A, p. 1.

[22] *Associated Press*, "Hunger frets 12-million families," *St. Petersburg Times*, November 1, 2003.

[23] Nicholas D. Kristof, "North Korean time bomb ticks away," *St. Petersburg Times*, April 22, 2004, Section A, p. 15.

[24] Jessica Stern, "How America created a terrorist haven," *New York Times* article printed in the *St. Petersburg Times*,

August 21, 2003, Section A, p. 16. Jessica Stern is the author of the book, *Terrorism in the Name of God: Why Religious Militants Kill.*

[25] Maureen Dowd, "Iraq nightmares are coming true," from *New York Times* news service printed in the *St. Petersburg Times*, August 21, 2003, Section A, p. 17.

[26] Jonathan Turley, "Care-package contents: body armor," *Los Angeles Times* printed in the *St. Petersburg Times*, October 4, 2003, Section A, p. 16.

[27]" Cheney: Kerry win risks terror attack," *CNN.com*, in which Cheney is quoted as saying, "If we make the wrong choice [electing John Kerry], then the danger is that we'll get hit again—that we'll be hit in a way that will be devastating from the standpoint of the United States. And then we'll fall back into the pre-9/11 mindset, if you will, that in fact these terrorist attacks are just criminal acts and that we're not really at war."

[28] See endnote 22.

[29] Richard Leiby and Dana Priest, "The Spy Next Door," *Washington Post*, printed in the *St. Petersburg Times*, October 12, 2003, Section D, p. 1.

[30] Thomas L. Friedman, "What Republicans should be saying," *New York Times News Service* printed in the *St. Petersburg Times*, October 24, 2003, Section A, p. 16.

[31]Kathy Kristof, "Government pension agency needs shoring up," *Los Angeles Times article* printed in the *St. Petersburg Times*, November 9, 2003.

[32]Ibid.

[33]"3 states plan to sue power plants," *New York Times* news wire printed in the *St. Petersburg Times*, November 9, 2003, Section A, p. 2.

See also, "New rules to dictate Clean Air inquiries," *New York Times* news wire printed in the *St. Petersburg Times*, November 6, 2003, Section A, p. 6.

Associated Press, "Court blocks Clean Air changes," which appeared in the *St. Petersburg Times*, December 25, 2003, Section A, p. 5.

[34]"New rules to dictate Clean Air inquiries." *New York Times* news wire printed in the *St. Petersburg Times*, November 6, 2003, Section A, p. 6.

[35]"Far fewer polluters punished, records show," *Knight Ridder Newspapers*, printed in the *St. Petersburg Times*, December 9, 2003, Section A, p. 3.

[36]*Associated Press*, "EPA may alter rules on mercury emissions," *St. Petersburg Times*, December 3, 2003, Section A, p. 5.

[37]"Mercury turns fishermen to politics," *Scripps Howard News Service* printed in the *St. Petersburg Times*, March 20, 2004, Section A, p. 25.

[38]Adrienne P. Samuels, "Seas in dire straits, expert warns," *St. Petersburg Times*, May 6, 2004.

[39]"Global warming could lead to mass extinctions, scientists say," *St. Petersburg Times*, January 8, 2004, Section A., p. 5.

[40]Ibid.

[41]*Associated Press*, "EPA: N.Y. misled on 9/11 air quality," *St. Petersburg Times*, August 23, 2003, Section A, p. 4.

[42]<u>Hamdi v. Rumsfeld</u>, 542 US _____(2004) and <u>Rasul v. Bush</u>, 542 US _____(2004).

[43]Ibid.

[44]Jeffrey Steinberg, "National Security Mandarins Assail Bush and Cheney," *Executive Intelligence Review*, June 25, 2004.

Laura Secor, "Diplomatic Dissent," *The Prospect*, June 23, 2004, can be found at *www.prospect.org*.

Askia Muhammad, "U.S. Foreign Policy Hijacked," *FCN Publishing*, July 2, 2004, can be located at *www.finalcall. com.*

[45]J. Horan, "Let's Welcome Back Married Priests," *U.S. Catholic Magazine*, February 1999, p. 25.

[46]Tim Drake, "In Media Letter, Priests Call for Optional Celibacy," *National Catholic Register*, Vol. 79, No. 34, August 31-September 6, 2003.

[47]See endnote 1.

[48]Letter from Father Tadeusz Pacholczyk to the *National Catholic Register*, which was in response to a reader's letter reacting to an interview with Father Pacholczyk. Letter was published in *National Catholic Register*, Vol. 79, No. 22, p. 8, June 1-7, 2003.

Father Tadeusz Pacholczyk, "The Wisdom of the Church is in Her Silence, Too," *National Catholic Register*, August 10-16, 2003.

Special quantity discounts are available on bulk purchases for educational use, fundraisers, and general resale. If you are interested in special bulk pricing, please contact :

Better World Together Publishing, Inc.
Post Office Box 2015
Palm Harbor, Florida 34682-2015

THE CATHOLIC CHALLENGE:
A Question of Conscience
By Thomas W. Rezanka

Copyright © 2004 by Thomas W. Rezanka
ISBN 0-9762100-0-2

ORDER FORM

To order individual copies of the book visit
www.thecatholicchallenge.com, or use this page as a mail
order form and send to :

Better World Together Publishing, Inc.
Post Office Box 2015
Palm Harbor, Florida 34682-2015

The Catholic Challenge: A Question of Conscience
ISBN: 0-9762100-0-2

_____ copies X $24.95 per copy=	$
Shipping for first copy	$ 3.85
Sales Tax ((x) .07 in Florida)	$
Shipping for add'l copies ($1.50 ea)	$
Handling	$ 1.45
Total	**$**

Use reverse side for shipping and payment instructions.
Please allow 2-4 weeks for U.S. Delivery. This offer is subject
to change without notice. International Orders should inquire
about shipping rates. Sorry, no cash or COD.

Ship to:

Name: _____

Address _____

City   _____

State _____ Zip _____-_____

Daytime phone (_____) _____-_____

Payment Method:

[ ] Check Enclosed

[ ] Money Order Enclosed

Credit Card Orders are accepted through

http://www.thecatholicchallenge.com